Other books by this author

The Adventures of Captain Heman Kenney and Lady Catherine 1833-1917

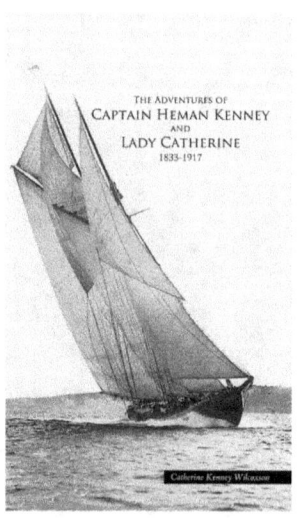

Open Doors and Open Windows:
A Journey with God

Catherine Kenney Wilcoxson

Copyright © 2017 All rights reserved.
Watt Light Publishing Company
404 LeBlanc Street
DeQuincy, LA 70633
Author's Email: cawilcoxson@theladycatherinecompany.com
Website: www.theladycatherinecompany.com

No part of this book may be reproduced or transmitted in any form or by any means, electronic or mechanical, including photocopying, recording or by any information storage and retrieval system, without written permission from the author.

Library of Congress Control Number: 2017909817

All Scripture quotations marked (NIV) are taken from the Holy Bible, New International Version®, NIV®. Copyright © 1973, 1978, 1984, 2011 by Biblica, Inc.™ Used by permission of Zondervan. All rights reserved worldwide. www.zondervan.com The "NIV" and "New International Version" are trademarks registered in the United States Patent and Trademark Office by Biblica, Inc.™ The "NIV" and "New International Version" are trademarks registered in the United States Patent and Trademark Office by Biblica, Inc.™

Publisher's Cataloging-in-Publication Data
Wilcoxson, Catherine 1952-
Open Doors and Open Windows: A Journey with God
Revised Updated Edition: First published 2011 Independent Publisher -ISBN 13: 978-1-4507-8910-3; PCN 2011936253
DeQuincy, Louisiana
Watt Light Publishing Company
350p
ISBN 978-0-9966807-3-8- Paperback
ISBN 978-0-9966807-4-5-- Ebook
Subjects: 1. Christianity – Jesus Christ, seeking, new life, change. 2. Love – rebounding after breakup, commitment, marital faithfulness. 3. Roots – family ties, pulling up roots, moving, changes, new friends. 4. Talents – discovery, using them, accountability. 5. Baptism – blood of Jesus, immersion in water, salvation, forgiveness, new life, transformation. 6. Travel - taking gospel message, planes, trains, cars, feet. 7. Weather – rain, sleet, snow, hurricanes. 8. Ministry – weddings, funerals, traditions, customs. 9. Fear – Belshazzar, confronting fear, mid-life changes, adjustment, life's problems, surgery, suffering

Summary: *Open Doors and Open Windows: A Journey with God* is a story about Catherine's own journey to find a personal relationship with God. It tells of her life as a girl, her experiences as a young adult, a broken heart and rescue by Paul, the man from Tennessee. Let the lessons Catherine learned from her love of God and life experiences make you aware of doors God may open in your life.

DEDICATION

I dedicate this book to

GOD.

Finding Him as a young adult was the best thing that ever happened to me.

ACKNOWLEDGMENTS

Thank You for the man from Tennessee, Paul my husband. He stood by me and walked with me through the opened doors that God set before me.

Paul was with me every step of the way while writing this book. I thank God for him daily.

Thank you, Dear.

Contents

DEDICATION V

ACKNOWLEDGMENTS VII

CHAPTER 1 SEARCH AND FIND 1

CHAPTER 2 STUDY ...DECISION ...CHANGE 13

CHAPTER 3 GREAT LAKES CHRISTIAN COLLEGE 29

CHAPTER 4 LOVE 43

CHAPTER 5 LIFE'S JOURNEY WITH PAUL 65

CHAPTER 6 WHAT ARE ROOTS? 87

CHAPTER 7 GOD-GIVEN TALENTS – YOURS AND MINE 107

CHAPTER 8 BAPTISM 121

CHAPTER 9 CARS, PLANES, TRAINS AND FEET 135

CHAPTER 10 WEATHER 159

CHAPTER 11 WEDDINGS 187

CHAPTER 12 FUNERALS 207

CHAPTER 13 TRADITIONS 237

CHAPTER 14 NEWBORN BABIES 255

CHAPTER 15 KNEE-KNOCKING FEAR 277

CHAPTER 16 – IT'S A WONDERFUL LIFE 297

CHAPTER 17 – NOW WHAT? 305

EPILOGUE: SIX YEARS LATER 347

ENDNOTES... 335

Catherine's Childhood Home
16 Rufus Avenue, Halifax, Nova Scotia, Canada

Chapter 1 Search and Find

I always liked church. As a child, my parents would take the whole family; I liked to sing along with the choir. The songs we sang were anthems and marches; however, I did not know what we were singing nor, why.

On Sunday mornings, the Kenney kids were up early, making sure they were ready to walk the half mile to St. Johns' church for Sunday school. I remember my father going to church regularly. For the first time since his childhood, my father was involved at this church. He had a friend, a Mr. Norman. They helped organize the yearly church picnic. I have fond memories of attending. I remember the steam rising from the dry ice used to make ice cream and the small toy that was given to the children. It resembled a Frisbee today but had string on both ends. You placed both hands on the string, pulled it and the disk would whistle. Something happened to hurt my father's feelings, and he stopped attending and just stayed home. I believe my father's responsibilities were given to others. However, my mother continued to take us to church. I do remember that my father would have dinner ready when we came home. In addition, I also remember it was very important to him that I was in Sunday school, and if I wanted, to go to church.

We only went to Sunday school and church in the fall winter and spring. I thought everyone took church off for the summer. Most of my family spent the summers at our cottage in Sheet Harbour. I was the middle child of six. My father would come down to the cottage from Halifax on Friday night and return on Sunday evening to work Monday, leaving Mother with the kids during the week. As far back as I can remember, he had four weeks' vacation and spent it all with us at the cottage.

Sundays were different from the rest of the days of the week. I can still remember my father telling us to be quiet. We were on our beach, which was right in front of our cottage. It was early in the morning and we were not allowed to raise our voices. My father said, "Don't you know it is Sunday? Your voices will carry down the Harbour, now be quiet." Maybe church for my father was quiet fortitude among nature. I never heard him speak of God or speak to God.

In my mind, only children, ministers, or priests could talk to God. I did not know any adults that talked to God. Only the minister or priest, and he read it from a book. It sounded like words you would speak to a president of the United States or Queen of England. I surely did not talk to anyone like that. However, small children were different. They were taught to say simple prayers that had rhymed like, "Now I lay me down to sleep. I pray the Lord my soul to keep. If I should die before I wake. I pray the Lord my soul to take. God, bless Mommy, Daddy, brothers and sisters" and whomever else you could put in there so you would not have to go to sleep. When you got a little older, you did not have to say that prayer any longer.

I was also taught that you were born in a church. Pick your denomination; it did not matter. If you were born into it, that was the end of it. You did not question it, and you certainly did not go to or visit other churches. God was at your church. You were required to take the time on Sunday morning to gather with those of the same persuasion. You were not important enough to ask any questions. Only the ones who wore the long robes, and the fancy braided rope, used for a belt, were important enough. The ones who carried the gold cross on a stick, as they walked up the aisle to the front of the church. You were expected to follow your little book of rules.

I was okay with all this. I liked to watch the pageantry around me. The organ was so loud it vibrated off the four walls and came right back at you. I watched the men and boys dressed in white robes up front. I always noticed the shiny black shoes that showed under their white robes. They walked from one spot to another. Each spot marked a place to say a blessing or a prayer. Then the voices of the people around me would answer all at the same time. I did not even know the priest had asked a question. Everyone knew when to stand up, when to sit down, and when to kneel on the prayer bench. That was the hardest for it hurt my knees.

My friend, Marilyn, who lived on Fredrick Avenue, just behind my house, was attending what she called an evangelistic church. We went to school together. Her parents allowed her to do things that my father would never let me get away with. She could stay out as long as she wanted. My mother would come looking for me.

I knew that she was born the same persuasion as my family. I actually asked her what she thought she was doing. She had better come back where she belonged. What does she mean she was studying the Bible? She should not lower herself to such a thing. Then she told me she liked it. She liked getting to know Jesus.

Search and Find

I was shocked. How can you get to know Jesus? Everyone knew that we were not good enough to have a personal relationship with Him. I never heard us sing "What a Friend We Have in Jesus" – only, "Onward Christian Solders" and maybe an anthem telling God how great He was. I was christened as a baby, confirmed as a young girl, questioning my faith as a teenager.

Tragedy struck my life at the age of twelve. My older brother of fourteen was killed in a car accident. Wade was hit by a car while leaving a dance in Sheet Harbour. The driver was a young man who had been drinking.

All I have to do is close my eyes, and I still have a very clear picture of what took place that night. The cabin in Sheet Harbour had two bedrooms. Dad built bunk beds under the small window in the living area. I slept on the top bunk; Blair, my younger brother, was on the lower bunk. I awoke hearing adults talking. They were sitting at the small kitchen table. My father was there, for it was a Saturday night. Also sitting there were my mother, a Royal Canadian Mounted Policeman, and a priest. I recognized him being a priest because he wore a white collar. When they realized I was awake, the priest asked my father if he should continue. My father said it was okay. I didn't say a word, for I knew my father would not approve of my interrupting an adult conversation. I listened carefully; they talked about someone involved in an accident.

Then there was a banging on the door. It was my aunt, uncle, and cousin Elry. They were totally upset. Crying and almost shouting, "I am so sorry about Wade."

My father took my mother into their bedroom for she seemed to be falling apart. I began to cry; everyone else was crying. However, I wasn't exactly sure why. Elry came over, put his arm around me, and said, "Don't worry; everything will be fine." My father sat down with me and told me that my brother had died. He was run over by a car. That night changed my life forever. My perfect world had changed.

For what is death? For me a twelve-year-old, it was tearing my life apart. I just kept thinking, "How could God do this? We go to church most Sundays. Doesn't God know that?"

A year later, a promise was kept to my mother. My father would take her home to visit her family. Her family was in Alberta, Canada; we lived in Halifax, Nova Scotia. She had not been home to see her family in twenty-five years. The death of my brother made life more fragile, more urgent. Now was the time for her to return home. However, how do you do that with six children?

At the time, I was attending a small group of teens for a Bible Study on Friday evenings. I did not attend for the Bible study; I had no interest in that, for I had never studied the Bible. I went for the get-togethers after the lesson. This group was at the preacher's house one night after the lesson. The subject of my parents' trip came up in conversation. I laughed and revealed that my parents had places for all their children to stay but me.

Ron and Rita, the young preacher and his wife, volunteered to take me in. My desperate parents were contacted. There was a dinner at my house and then a dinner at Ron and Rita's house, and a week later, my parents left for their four-week trip to Alberta.

Throughout July, I met people who studied the Bible, prayed and called themselves "Christians." They were people that loved and cared for each other. Church was a lot different from what I was used to. You did not walk into a quiet, cold building among strangers. Here there was talking and fellowship. The worship was warm and happy. The preacher talked about Jesus. Jesus actually cared about people, all people, and what I found interesting was that Jesus even cared about me. I knew something was different and I liked it.

Over the next three years, I tried to attend this church whenever I could. It was not easy. My father forbade it. I was expected to be at our church on Sunday from 10:00 a.m. until 11:00 a.m. The 11:00 a.m. to 12 noon service was optional. That was my chance to skip out and make my way to the church I wanted to attend. I could get there if I walked fast. Sometimes my Sunday school teacher offered me a ride. I needed that ride, but how could I tell her I was going to another church? I did not; I asked her to drop me off a block from the church. I had many more friends at this church, and I was learning more about Jesus. The span of three years passed. I decided I wanted to do what Jesus was asking me to do, and His words went right to my heart.

> **Come to me, all you who are weary and burdened, and I will give you rest. Take my yoke upon you and learn from me, for I am gentle and humble in heart, and you will find rest for your souls. For my yoke is easy and my burden is light.**[1]

How could I even think of doing anything? I was not even sixteen years old. My father would not be pleased.

Oh, believe me; I know how one feels when they make the decision to follow Jesus or to reject the whole thing. The seed of God's Word was growing in my heart. No one put it there. No one told me what I had to do. I knew what I had to do. Nevertheless, was I willing?

I had an argument with myself daily. "You have got to be kidding me," I would tell myself. "Do you really know what will happen if I do such a thing? Maybe I just need to go to my priest and ask him what to do."

Search and Find

I did and that was a disaster. The questions I had. He did not even look at them. "Don't you worry about questions," he said. "Just come on Sunday morning and bring your gift offering with you. Do you have a church bank? Here, take this one." He handed me a cardboard church building with a hole in the top. "Make sure you have it full by Easter." Then I found myself out the door.

Now what do I do? I was more confused than ever. I just let things continue the way they were.

Search and Find

Dear God,

Thank You for allowing me to question my faith.

Thank You for allowing me to meet people that opened the Bible to me. Your word is alive and has begun to grow inside my heart.

Thank You for not giving up on me. It scares me to think of the path I would have taken if I had not been pointed Your way.

Thank You for being with me at the beginning of my journey to know You.

Thank You, Thank You, Thank You, Thank You.

In Jesus Name I pray,

Cathy Kenney

**Entrance to Church of Christ Building,
48 Convoy Avenue, Halifax, Nova Scotia, Canada**

CHAPTER 2 STUDY ...DECISION ...CHANGE

A study of more than three years brought me right back to the discussion I had with Marilyn, my young friend, years before. Her statement remained with me all this time. She liked getting to know Jesus. I found out I liked it too. This business of being a Christian was all right. I enjoyed being around Christians. They were kind, helpful and caring to all those they met.

I still did not know very much about the Bible. The stories of Jesus got most of my attention. The songs they sang to Him made me feel good. Before I knew it, the scriptures were speaking to me right into my heart. I felt like I was standing amongst the crowd looking up to Peter, as he told the story of how we all crucified Jesus. Mankind did not accept God's Son. Instead, they hung Him on a tree.

However, what really amazed me was that this was God's plan.

Jesus was to die on the cross and on the third day rise up from the hands of death. Death could not keep Him. The death was to wipe away all sin. Rising from the dead was a new beginning. Our sins were taken away. The wall that separated people from God was knocked down.

I was among the people to whom Peter was talking. I listened as he explained what man did. When the people heard this, when I heard this, they were cut to the heart. I was cut to the heart. They asked Peter, "Brothers, what shall we do?" I asked Peter, "What shall I do?"

"Peter replied, 'Repent and be baptized every one of you, in the name of Jesus Christ for the forgiveness of your sins. And you will receive the gift of the Holy Spirit.' With many other words he warned them, and he pleaded with them, 'Save yourself from the corrupt generation.' Those who accepted his message were baptized and about three thousand were added to their number that day."

Doesn't Peter know that I was baptized as a baby? How can a baby repent? Repent of what? I do not remember ever receiving any Holy Spirit. Looks like three thousand did what Peter asked. No mention of babies anywhere. The three thousand were old enough to make a decision. I did not make any decision. Does confirmation count for anything? I attended classes at around age twelve. I do not remember a thing I was taught. All I remember is wearing a pretty white dress, with white socks and white shoes. I remember the Bishop was there. He wore a pointed hat and white robe with gold trimming. Two girls went to the front together; he placed one hand on each of our heads, and then we returned to our seats. However, nothing was said about repenting, baptism, forgiveness of sin, or the gift of the Holy Spirit.

The Apostle Peter continued to speak and everyone continued to listen. I continued to listen. Peter had many other words he was using to warn them, warn me! What were the other words?

Peter continued, "Save yourself!" I have to save myself. My mother can't save me, my priest can't save me, my preacher friends can't save me. I have to save myself. I found the other words He used to warn them throughout the scripture. One of my favorites was:

> "Ask and it will be given to you, seek and you will find; knock and the door will be opened to you. For everyone who asks receives; he who seeks finds; and to him who knocks the door will be opened."[2]

Therefore, I am ready to ask, seek, find and knock. Even though I wanted to do what Jesus said, I had a big problem, my father. However, I could not carry the burden alone any longer. The burden that kept me awake at night. I shared it with Ron Pauls and Walter Hart, two preachers. Ron Pauls and his wife Rita were very close to me. After staying with them for one month while my parents were away, they became like family. Both of these men were happy with my decision, but again, what to do about my father? They agreed to go and speak to him on my behalf. The meeting with my father lasted more than three hours.

At midnight on a cold January night, my parents came to the church to witness my baptism into Christ. You will have to realize how unusual this was. My father didn't go anywhere in the winter. He put his car in the family garage and it would stay there until spring.

This particular January night was cold and icy with fresh snow on the ground. I remember it well. I also remember wondering how they were going to get up Main Avenue because the road was so icy.

I was with Rita at her house. A phone call came, asking her to take me to the church building for my parents were coming to the baptism. I was shocked. "Are you sure?" I asked Rita.

Ron also said, "Prepare for the baptism and keep Cathy out of sight." I didn't see my parents when they arrived.

As I walked up the steps to the baptistery, Ron was on the other side. The people sitting in the pews could not see us yet. I heard a, "Psst. Psst." Ron was quietly trying to get my attention. "The water is very cold; do not scream!"

Ron had a whole lot of respect for my father. The last thing he wanted my father to hear that night was my scream. Afterward he came to me, wrapped scarves around me, and put a hat on my head. "I don't want to hear your father's reaction if you catch a cold." I just smiled.

I was being immersed into Jesus. This is what I wanted. I was being buried; Jesus was buried in His tomb. When I came up out of that cold water, I arose like Jesus. My sins were washed away, I was clean, and I was beginning a new life, a life with Jesus.

To this day, I have no idea what was said at that meeting with my father. Nevertheless, I do remember clearly that I was the one who had to go home and live with my family.

My father was not happy. He made it clear that he did not understand why the church that his parents and grandparents were members of was not good enough for me. Furthermore, if I were going to this other church, I would have to find my own way there, because he certainly was not taking me. By the way, he said, "On Sundays, before you leave the house, your room is to be clean and the kitchen cleaned up." I felt a little like Cinderella.

Oh, dear, what have I done? Would it not have been better just to attend church like before, when no one knew?

Not only that, but the priest had taken me aside just a few weeks before. He was wondering why my name was on a young people's bulletin from another church, and why I wrote an article inside. I never did find out how he got hold of the bulletin the teenagers had put out. It was the teenagers from my Friday night group, and at a church, I was not supposed to be attending. I had really stirred things up.

Things got worse. A young woman, Ron Paul's sister Eleanor, sent me a postcard congratulating me on becoming a Christian. I did not know anything about it until sitting down with the family for dinner. There on the dinner plate was my postcard. My father said, "Read it."

I read, "Dear Cathy, I am so happy you have become a Christian. . ."

My older brother, Barry, and sisters, Lois and Marlane, questioned, "Do you think we aren't Christians?" My father just allowed them to drill me.

How could I answer such a question?

This was a very hard time for me. Questioning my own faith had turned me into an outcast from my family. After several months of Sunday mornings, cleaning my room and doing dishes before my ride appeared to take me to worship, something changed.

One thing that changed was me. I was a nicer person. I did not get into trouble of any kind.

Second, my father noticed.

Study . . . Decision . . . Change

I remember the Sunday morning well. I was having a hard time getting out of bed. I was thinking, "I will be late if I don't get up. It really doesn't matter if I miss one Sunday." Then I heard a voice. Maybe it was God Himself calling my name. No, it was not God; it was my father.

"Catherine, are you getting up? You will be late for church."

The battle was over. From that time on, I was free to worship God.

Why did my father give me such a hard time? There may have been several reasons, but one of the main reasons was he thought I was getting involved in some kind of cult. He didn't know anything about the church. I believe he was protecting me because he loved me. He had changed his mind, not that he agreed with me, but he was beginning to respect my decision.

Perseverance. Keep on keeping on, strength, focused; having a plan, staying power, and sticking to it, never give up. Persistence and being patient, continuing in a course of action, in spite of difficulty or lack of success. God never wants you to give up. It may not be easy, but He never said it would.

"For this reason . . ."

What reason?

The divine power He has given is everything we need for life.

"So for this reason, make every effort to add to your faith goodness; and to goodness, knowledge; and to knowledge, self-control; and to self-control, perseverance; and to perseverance, godliness; and to godliness, brotherly kindness; and to brotherly kindness, love. For if you possess these qualities in increasing measure, they will keep you from being ineffective and unproductive in your knowledge of our Lord Jesus Christ. But if anyone does not have them, he is nearsighted and blind, and has forgotten that he has been cleansed from his past sins."[3]

And.

"Therefore, since we have been justified through faith we have peace with God through our Lord Jesus Christ, through whom we have gained access by faith into this grace in which we now stand. And we rejoice in the hope of the glory of God. Not only so, but we also rejoice in our sufferings, because we know that suffering produces perseverance; perseverance, character; and character, hope. And hope does not disappoint us, because God has poured out his love into our hearts by the Holy Spirit, whom he has given us."[4]

My life had changed. I now knew who I was and I had hope. God loved me and He would walk by my side for my life's journey. God always opens doors. If we look for them, we can find them. I saw the doors wide open and ran through.

*****

The preachers that helped me and whom I depended upon moved away. Like preachers do, they come and go. That is just life I was told, like winter to spring, or rain and sunshine; life moves on. Nevertheless, was I ready to be out there by myself? I was afraid and pleaded to this new God of mine. Would I fall back into the world I was a part of two short years before?

Sin. Sin can be overpowering. Sin is an immoral act considered to violate divine law. An act regarded as a serious offence. It is a noun and a verb when acted upon. Sin violates the law of God. It separates you from Him. It is evil doing and a fall.

> "Your iniquities have separated you from your God; your sins have hidden his face from you so that he will not hear."[5]

> ". . . but each one is tempted when, by his own evil desire, he is dragged away and enticed. Then, after desire has conceived, it

gives birth to sin; and sin, when it is full-grown, gives birth to death."[6]

I was good at sin. Remember how I started this journey? No one even knew I was attending worship services all those years. I would go to Sunday school, where my father insisted I would be. However, I saw loopholes and used them to my own advantage. I was sneaky, the best there was. Just ask my friends at the time. They would tell you I was good at smoking a cigarette, and my mother never knew it. If I wanted to be out on the street with my friends, I would. It did not matter that the stick was waiting for me when I got back home. I did what I wanted to do when I wanted to do it. My poor mother, she used the stick on me more than once.

But I had changed; Jesus changed me. Would I fall apart not having a support group? Whom did I have to talk to? No one. God knew it. God opened another door: An invitation to visit with Ron and Rita Pauls, the preacher that just moved away.

A funny thing about these doors that God opens is that it is hard to go through them. I took every babysitting job I could find for the month of July and most of August. I saved every cent and bought a plane ticket to Ontario.

I had never been out of Nova Scotia. I got on a plane by myself. I didn't even know how to buckle the seatbelt. There in Ontario, I met more people who called themselves

"Christian." I was there one week. I prayed to God, "Why show me this if I have to go back?" I was afraid I would fall back into my old lifestyle. I did not want that lifestyle. What was I to do?

God opened another door.

Ron Pauls asked, "Why don't you stay and go to school here?"

I called my parents and told them I wanted to attend Great Lakes Christian College. I had two things on my side.

One – God.

Two – My parents wanted to retire and did not know what they were going to do with me. Sound familiar?

I remember thinking, "This new God of mine really does care. He really answers prayer."

It was almost as if God was asking me, "What else do you want?"

"I don't know, God, but please stand by; I will be back to you." I did not know what I needed, but God did.

God really answers prayer. Not, "Can I have a new car prayer?" Nevertheless, if you are his child and you are depending on Him, He will be there.

Study . . . Decision . . . Change

Dear Father in Heaven,

Thank You for sending Your Son, Jesus Christ.

I am learning more and more each day of the stories of how your Son lived here on this earth. Stories You left us about why You sent Him here.

Thank You for the people I have gotten to know. They call themselves Christians. It always amazes me how much they care for me.

I am learning about Your follower, Peter. Peter was quite the character. He never was quite sure of what he was doing or what he would do. There is no question he loved Your Son Jesus and would stand by Him, no matter what happened.

I can relate to Peter. I never know what to do. You know my situation. If I break away from my earthly father's beliefs, I would hurt him. I love my father. I also know he will not be very happy.

Thank You for being with Ron Pauls and Water Hart. It was not easy for them to talk with my father. But I believe You were in that room with them.

Thank You for Your Son Jesus, whom You sent for me!

I will always remember that night I was buried with Jesus in baptism. Raised again, a new birth. Jesus is my Savior.

Like Peter, I will follow Him and stand by Him no matter whatever happens.

Be with me, God, on this new journey.

Cathy Kenney

Great Lakes Christian College, Beamsville, Ontario, Canada

CHAPTER 3 GREAT LAKES CHRISTIAN COLLEGE

It is not a college at all but a high school. All private schools in Canada once were called "colleges." It did not matter if you were in kindergarten or second-year university.

GLCC was operated by the church I attended. There were less than two hundred students. Most of the students lived in dormitories. Some were day students and others were five-day students who went home on weekends. Then there were seven-day students who stayed until school ended in late spring. I was a five-day student. The girls' dorm was the mansion or the main house on the estate that covered several hundred acres. It was old and it was beautiful. The boys' dorm was the old stone chicken coop. No kidding. They would still see feathers gliding through the air occasionally. Several other buildings were built on the estate, including a school building and two residences for those taking care of the students.

What have I just done? I now am by myself. Have I just cut ties with my family? They are now going to be twelve hundred miles away. Do I hate my family? Of course, not, I love my family dearly and I believe they love me. To me, my future was serving the new God I was getting to know. I would follow Him wherever He led me. I would make wise decisions, and I would not have anyone tell me what to do.

I was given the choice of moving into the girl's dorm that very night or waiting until the next morning. I chose to go into the dorm that very night. I was afraid I would lose my nerve by morning.

My dear friends, Ron and Rita, whom I was visiting, quickly came up with sheets, blankets, pillow, towels and many things I cannot remember. Everything I would ever need. I was dropped off at the entryway of the girls' dorm with my suitcase. There was a lot of activity in the "Common room," a very large living room of the mansion. Mrs. Mower, my dorm mother, was waiting for me. So was this guy who wanted to be the first to meet me. Bill Bartlett asked my name. I quietly answered, "Cathy."

"I hear you are from Halifax, Nova Scotia. Then I will call you "Halifax." Bartlett and I are friends to this day. In fact, he and his sweet wife Becky live one hour from

Covington in Greencastle, Indiana. We have all become good friends.

  I had two roommates, Bonnie and Melanie. Our room was on the third floor of the mansion. These roommates were good for me. They were surprised when I arrived with just a small suitcase. Back home my mom and my sister Marlane packed my clothes and bought things I would need and send them to me. My memories to this day are ones full of love for these two girls. School started the next day, and I did not even know where the front door was. My grade 12 was about to begin.

  Of course, the next day I stayed lost most of the time. Everyone seemed friendly and would point the way. However, after one bell rang, I found myself alone in the hallway. I had no idea where everyone went. Turns out I was not told about chapel. I hardly even knew what chapel was. In the middle of school, we were going to worship! An adult found me wandering the hallway and pointed the way to chapel. As I entered, of course, I was late, and everyone laughed. Every year they wanted to know who would be the first one late for chapel. Unfortunately, that was I. Me! I quickly found an empty spot on a bench and tried to hide. I soon forgot the embarrassment when the students began to sing. The a cappella singing was beautiful; I thought I had died and gone to heaven. God was certainly in this place. Chapel became my favourite time of day.

  The students ate breakfast, lunch, and dinner together. Then we had study hall before we had free time and could go back to the dorm. It did not take long for lifelong relationships to be made.

I missed my family. I was allowed a phone call once a month for about 20 minutes. This was my father's rule and I just accepted it. I had so much to tell them when I called. I remember my parents' phone number only had three digits. I had to go through a special telephone operator to connect me to the small village of Sheet Harbour, Nova Scotia, where my family now lived.

I fell in love with Bill. Not Bill Bartlett, but his best friend, Bill. He was Christian; he gave me my first Bible. He taught me to sing the new songs. We would go to church together. We would take long walks, it did not matter that it was the middle of winter. Bill was not anything like the other guys I knew. He seemed to be kind all the time. We were in chorus together. He sang bass, I sang soprano. The chorus traveled in an old yellow school bus on a spring break trip to the United States. This was all new to a girl who had never been a hundred miles away from home before coming to Ontario. I sent a very long letter, more like a diary, telling my mother all about the trip. She said it took her a whole day to read it. She sent it to the church in Fairview and my friends passed it around. They enjoyed my special chorus trip as well.

Summer came; everyone went home. I went back to Nova Scotia. I did not know how, but somehow I would go back to Great Lakes. GLCC offered grade 13 at that time. I did not have the money to return. People from the church in

Fairview helped me with expenses the previous year, but what about the next. I had worked in the kitchen to help pay for my tuition. I found out that was not going to be possible for the next year. I was required to have surgery on my left foot. Surgery was nothing new to me. (That story is told in another chapter.) I wrote a letter to a Mr. Flemming, who lived in Beamsville, where GLCC was located. He was a successful businessman, who raised baby chicks for the chicken industry in Ontario. I knew that he helped students to attend Great Lakes. He agreed to help me and would pay my tuition; and when I was finished, I would pay it back to the school in full. I was back at school by the middle of September. Late but I was back.

Things were not as easy for me that year. First, I had to use crutches because of my foot. I was not permitted to be on the third floor of the dorm. I had roommates who were a lot younger than I was. Because of my late arrival at school, I was behind in schoolwork. I never seemed to be able to catch up. Then I found out that some Christians were not as Christian as I thought. I was falling through the cracks.

The teachers did not give me the extra help that I needed. I was struggling and felt I was drowning and had a hard time keeping my head above water. I was alone, and my Christian brothers and sisters did not seem to notice. I did not have the help I needed, and some people were playing foul ball. To make matters worse, I needed more surgery on my foot. I did not want to go back to Nova Scotia to have this done. I wanted to finish my last year of school. It was arranged that I would have the operation in Ontario, at a hospital close to the school. I had to find a place to recuperate from surgery. I could not return to the dorm. Three options were in front of me. I could stay with Ron and Rita and their family, stay with my aunt Alice (my mother's sister in Niagara on the Lake), or take the invitation by Bill's parents that I stay with them, while Bill was at school. I chose Bill's parents. That was perfect; I would see Bill on the weekends. I needed three weeks to recover before I could return to school.

When I look back at the week I spent at Bill's home, I get nightmares. They were the meanest people I had ever met. This surprised me, for I had met them before and even spent a weekend there with Bill. However, behind closed doors, the nightmare began. I was expected to keep my room clean every day. I was expected to be downstairs for every meal when called. I was made to walk to church four blocks. On the surface, that may not sound unreasonable, but I had just gone through bone surgery. I was on crutches and very weak. If my doctors had known what I was doing, they would have been fit to be tied.

I remember being afraid. I dreaded hearing, "Cathy, lunch is ready, come down to the kitchen." Having to make my way down the stairs from my bedroom to the kitchen was slow and painful. I would hear "Are you coming? Don't be so slow." Conversation was sparse, to say the least during lunch. They asked questions of my past, and they couldn't understand how my parents would allow me to have surgery away from home.

To tell you the truth, I couldn't completely understand that either. However, it wasn't their idea. It was mine because I didn't want to miss another year of school. I just didn't know how hard it would be.

The fifth day I was there; they entered my room and informed me that I was no longer welcome there. They wanted me out of the house by the end of the day.

You know that I did not even cry. I turned to God and talked to Him for a while. I told Him I had no idea what was going on, nor why. This man, Bert, who said I was no longer welcome in his house, was a preacher. "Make me understand, God, and help me know what to do next." I could not call Ron; I felt like he might not believe me, for I was still just a kid. Who would believe it? I would not believe it, if it were told to me. I called my aunt Alice, who lived about an hour away. I told her I really needed her help; she was there in less than two hours. My things were on the front lawn. I climbed into her car and she took me home.

My Aunt Alice told her sister Doris, my mother how she found me. "A Christian?" my mother said. "If he is a Christian, then I don't want to be one." It took over twenty years for my mother to get past the fact that a Christian could act this way.

From that day on, Bill's parents did everything in their power to break us up. He was forbidden to see me. If he did not abide by their wishes, then they would bring him home from Great Lakes Christian College.

Two weeks later, when I returned to school, Bill was waiting for me. He said that he was quitting school and separating from his parents. He wanted to be with me. I thought this all was very interesting. Nevertheless, common sense told me he was not leaving school for me. There were three months left in the final semester. We would just break up until then, which we did. I thought it was hard before, now I had to do everything by myself. I began to question God, "What has gone wrong?" This was one of the times in my life that I felt very lonely. I left a life behind; only to find out I really did not have a life in front of me. Again, to make matters worse, Bill broke up with me in June. No reason given and I had no idea why. All I knew was that his parents had won. I was broken and tired. I went home to Nova Scotia.

I did not really blame God. I do not know why. I figured if Jesus could go to the wilderness and be tempted, then why not me? I believed it was Satan. I did not know what God had planned for me, but I certainly was in the wait-and-pray mode.

Christian friends in Nova Scotia were drawn into the fiasco of Bill's family. Bill's sister and her husband were visiting Nova Scotia, and they tried to find what negative things they could say about me. To this day, thirty-six years later, his family has tried to use me to get information about Bill. I have to be careful on Facebook who I accept as friends. "No, Brian, I will not accept you, for I don't trust you." But back then I just tried to pick up the pieces of my life and move forward. My friends rallied around me, and I found a job at Dalhousie University in downtown Halifax. I boarded with George and Pat Mansfield, the preacher and his family. It was my first real job, which gave me money to take a trip to Texas that summer.

I wrote a secret letter to Bill. I hoped he would respond by the time I returned. If he really wanted to see me, he would do it by then. He did not, and I tore him out of my heart, which left a hole the size grapefruit. My life would continue and I believed God would show me the way.

I thought my life would be perfect. I had God on my side. Everything was looking good there for a long time. If you think living a Christian life will get you a free ticket to a wonderful life with everything coming up roses, you are mistaken. You have forgotten one big thing. Satan rules this world. The more Christ-like your life becomes, the more he will be after you. Is that going to make you give up on God? Is it worth it? You try your hardest and bad things happen. Try harder. Better still, you need to have an unconditional love for Jesus, and let Satan know it. It does not matter what Satan does. The list can be endless. "Go ahead, Satan, bring it on. I will not forsake my God. Go and bother someone else, because you are wasting your time on me. That is it period."

Divorce. It cries out with a loud message. The dictionary identifies it as "a means of separation. Parting of the way, separate, split, break up, split up, detach or dissociate (something from)." To this day, I believe I went through a divorce before I was even married. I would never allow it to happen again.

Divorce is one of the worst words in the English dictionary. It destroys people. It is the opposite of love. That is why God hates it, and He warns us, His children, to stay away from it.

> "'I hate divorce,' says the Lord God of Israel . . ."[7]

How can God approve of divorce when it is the opposite of love, and God is love? Every church where we have worked, we have dealt with divorce. Many tears have fallen. Many hearts have been broken. Couples do things they would never dream of doing. Ask anyone who has gone through a divorce if they would recommend it to their friends, family or loved ones. I am sure you know the answer to that one. Divorce is the opposite of love. God is love. So what does that tell you?

Let me tell you what makes me sad about this whole thing about divorce. Man has stepped in and has declared it the unforgivable sin. God does not give up on anyone, including those who have a history of divorce. Divorce is so prevalent in our society today. Satan has used divorce as a great weapon to separate people from God. What is the answer? The teaching of what real marriage is. God made marriage; He did not make divorce. Education at an early age will help. We need to teach young people how to make wise decisions when picking one's mate.

*****

I spent the next four months healing. When I talked to God, I believed His answer was to be patient. Everything will turn out for good.

> **"And we know that in all things God works for the good of those who love him, who have been called according to his purpose."** [8]

Close to the end of November, God sent me His answer. I did not know for a while that it was His answer, but it was. I met Paul.

Dear God,

You know what I need before I do. You are always one, two, three, or more steps ahead of me. For this, I am grateful and thankful. Without Your presence at this time, I would be terrified. I can do things because You open doors. Give me the strength to go through.

Thank You for allowing me to attend GLCC. It was a new world to me. Thank You for Bonnie and Melanie. I do not think they realize how much I learn from them.

Thank You for Bill. I now have this wonderful Bible. It is not just a Bible; it is a beautiful black leather Bible. I promise I will study it well. Bill is so kind and He loves You too.

I pray for Bill's family. I do not know how to pray for them, but I pray hard.

Forgive me if I do not like them very well.

Thank You for my Aunt Alice. She rescued me from Bill's front yard. It did not matter to her what had happened; she was there for me. She took care of me until I was strong enough to return to school.

But God, Why?

My heart is broken – I will give it to you.

I pray all of this in Your Son's name.

Cathy Kenney

Our Wedding

CHAPTER 4 LOVE

Love is a good four-letter word. Four-letter words have a bad rap. There are so many bad four-letter words; it is hard to believe a four-letter word can be this good, however, it is.

"Love an intense feeling of deep affection. A great interest and pleasure in something." There are different kinds of love. We say we love ice cream. We love our best friend's dress. We even love to take a shower after working in the garden all day. We love our pets. Paul and I have raised five cats to old age and natural death. I will never forget them. Jack and Jill came first and then Sissy. Tinker and Belle came next. Christopher received Tinker in the first grade, and Jennifer was in the fifth grade with Belle. Those cats knew to whom they belonged. They lived for seventeen years. Our children would not remember their childhood without their best friends.

Blake came during the time of Tinker and Belle. He thought he was a cat and tried to clean himself with his tongue. However, he was an American Cocker Spaniel, born in Pittsburgh, Pennsylvania. He was the cutest puppy that I have ever seen. Paul did not want a dog, but he was out voted three to one. It turned out that Blake and Paul became great friends. Even Paul would tell you he was the smartest dog he ever knew. He understood the English language, or at least 40 words of it. He could do tricks that people could not believe. He had over 24 toy animals, each with a different name. You tell him to go get Monkey and he could do that. If you told him to get Elephant, he could dig to the bottom of his box and find it. He never chewed his animals, but carefully carried them in his mouth. Blake loved small children and because of that, he helped us out with Vacation Bible School for many years. Yes, we loved that dog. He lived to be fourteen, and it broke our hearts to have him put to sleep. Love can hurt.

We love our children. What parent does not love his children? God's greatest gift was His Son.

"For God so loved the world that he gave his one and only Son, that whoever believes in him shall not perish but have eternal life."[9]

God is love and has given people a great gift, the ability to love. Paul and I love our children. We thank God for them daily. God has shown us another kind of love, the love we have for our four grandchildren. What a blessing they are.

God is the creator of love. This is His plan.

> "If I speak in the tongues of men and of angels, but have not love, I am a noisy gong or a clanging cymbal. And if I have prophetic powers, and understand all mysteries and all knowledge, and if I have all faith, so as to remove mountains, but have not love, I am nothing. If I give away all I have, and if I deliver my body to be burned, but have not love, I gain nothing."

> "Love is patient and kind; love is not jealous or boastful; it is not arrogant or rude. Love does not insist on its own way; it is not irritable or resentful; it does not rejoice at wrong, but rejoices in the right. Love bears all things, believes all things, hopes all things, endures all things."

> "Love never ends; as for prophecies, they will pass away; as for tongues, they will cease; as for knowledge, it will pass away. For our

knowledge is imperfect and our prophecy is imperfect; but when the perfect comes, the imperfect will pass away. When I was a child, I reasoned like a child; when I became a man, I gave up childish ways. For now we see in a mirror dimly, but then face to face. Now I know in part; then I shall understand fully, even as I have been fully understood. So faith, hope, love abide, these three; but the greatest of these is love."[10]

However, the greatest love, second only to the love we have for God is love between a husband and wife. Back in the late fall of 1974, God sent me Paul. My life was broken, and my answer to prayer at the time was patience. When I resigned to the fact it did not matter, I would continue to live my life the way it was and put God in charge. In His time, not mine, I would know what to do. In the meantime, I would just wait. Every time I let God take over is when things began to happen.

Two brothers showed up from Tennessee. I did not even know they were expected. Paul would be staying as a preacher to a small church about thirty minutes from where I was living. Russell was flying back to Tennessee. His job was complete. He helped his brother drive his belongings to his new church.

To this day, the family joke is that, at that time, I wished that Russell were the one who was staying and Paul was the one going home. But thirty-six years later, I am glad Paul stayed.

Christmas was upon us. I planned to go to Sheet Harbour to be with my family. It was only an hour's drive away. I thought Paul, being new in the area, might feel a little lonely on Christmas Day. I invited him to have Christmas dinner with my family in Sheet Harbour. A few days later, George took me aside and told me I had a problem. He thought it was the funniest thing that could ever happen, but I had a big problem.

"What kind of problem do I have?" I asked.

"Paul thinks he has been invited for a week."

"A week?" I replied. "I invited him for Christmas dinner."

"He thinks you said a week."

"How can that be? I only told him I would be with my parents a week."

"That's how."

My good friends, George and Pat thought it was very funny. I thought, "Now what am I going to do? There is no room at my parents' house. We are already counting on using floor space for sleeping as it is." You know what they say; when you are in trouble, call your mother. That is what I did. It does not bother large families to have one extra person around.

My mother said, "Bring him; we will give him a good place on the floor."

God had to have something to do with this. How else did this stranger fit into my family so well? We went for walks in the snow. To this day Paul refers to this, as the day he fell in love with me walking in a winter wonderland. We walked on the frozen Harbour, something he really was not too sure of. We talked and talked and talked some more. Yes, we talked about Bill. Paul knew how wounded I was. After the Christmas holidays, he spent a large amount of his time at the home of George and Pat. He was not there to visit them; he was there to see me. I knew that he was getting serious, way too serious, way too fast. I kept thinking rebound, rebound. It had only been eight months since the break with Bill. However, everything seemed to be right. I had no fears of going into a relationship with Paul. It was as if God were opening another door. I have seen those doors before. Was I brave enough to go through? Did I have enough faith in God to believe this was His open door? All I knew was that I wanted to serve God. Paul was serving God already; I could just join him. Did I love him? He told me he had been looking for me for years. He loved me. I loved him as much as a broken heart could love. Paul told me he would take care of me. I believed him. Twenty-eight days after we had met, Paul asked me to marry him. On the front pew of the church building on 48 Convoy Avenue, Fairview, he asked me to be his wife. God opened a door and I went through. My answer was, "Yes, I will be your wife."

Did eyebrows rise? Many. Everyone was surprised and a little nervous. I believed that we had three things going our way. One – We both believed in God. We both loved that God and wanted to serve Him. Two – We were not 16 years old. Three – We were together every free minute we had.

We talked a long time with George. I guess you could call it marriage counseling. We told him he could announce it at church. George waited until services were over and chose the potluck dinner for the time of the announcement. He waited until everyone was seated and were eating. George stood and said he had an announcement. "Paul and Cathy are engaged to be married." Then he sat down. Most people had their mouths full of food, and most people knew Paul had only been in town for one month. Choking and coughing could be heard, before the well-wishes and congratulations began to be received.

The eyebrows that went up the highest were Ron Pauls'. He was like a father to me and he was not sure of the decision I was making. Being in Ontario, he didn't know Paul, and he was going to do some investigating.

Back in Nashville, Tennessee, where Paul was being supported, eyebrows were being raised as well. Jimmy Doris, a preacher who took Paul under his wing and helped him come to Nova Scotia to be a missionary, was very worried. What was going on in Nova Scotia? Paul was only there a month and now he was engaged to be married. Who was this Cathy?

It just so happened about a month later Abilene Christian College in Texas was having a Bible lectureship. Ron Pauls and Jimmy Doris were attending. When they saw each other across the room, they both headed for each other. Jimmy knowing Ron was from Canada and Ron knowing Jimmy was from Nashville they both asked the same question, almost at the same time.

"Who is this Cathy?"

Ron replied, "Better still who is this Paul Wilcoxson?" Both gentlemen felt better after having a long talk.

A July wedding began to be planned. We had no money for a wedding. I certainly was not marrying Paul for his money. My job was enough to keep me from starving, but not a lot left over to party. I had health problems again.

Health. This word contains a lot of information. It means the state of being free from illness or injury. Feeling whole or having well-being. We all ask the question regularly, "How are you?" It happened even in scripture.

> "'Dear friend, I pray that you may enjoy good health and that all my go well with you, even as your soul is getting along well.'"[11]

Good health, bad health – there is a big difference between the two. I was born with bad health. It did not show up until the age of ten or twelve, the years you grow the most. My legs were not working quite as they should. They gave out on me, with little warning.

Pain. It can be a noun or a verb. Pain that causes anguish is a verb. Pain that is anguish or that makes one miserable is a noun. It is a symptom of some physical hurt or disorder. It is a strongly unpleasant bodily sensation such as is caused by illness or injury." Pain is not fun, just ask anyone. It causes grief, sorrow, torment, torture and it makes one ache. Just ask Job.

> "Then they sat on the ground with him for seven days and seven nights. No one said a word to him, because they saw how great his suffering was."[12]

Pain is what I had every night. I was diagnosed with a bone condition called Diaphyseal Aclasis. I will leave it for you to look it up for in depth information. However, the short version is this: the end of my bones, just before the joints, grew in both directions. Anywhere I bend, I have knots or bumps growing out from my bones. I have a deformed left foot. Up to this point in my life, I have had five operations. Bones had to be removed in my leg and feet because it caused poor circulation and tendon problems. Without the surgery, I would not be able to walk. If you met me on the street or in the mall, you would never know I carried around this health issue. I look normal in every way. I have good doctors who fix it and I go on my way.

When Paul came into my life, I was recovering from the most recent operation. I had two ribs removed. The knots of bone growing on my ribs dug into my lung, and I could not straighten up. However, I was recovering nicely. That is until I started planning a wedding. I never knew I had so many friends. Friends who wanted to come to my wedding, the large wedding I was not going to have. The wedding kept growing and growing. My recovery slowed to a snail's pace. Seems I was having a hard time breathing.

Have you ever been to a checkup with your doctor and he asked the question, "How are you doing?"

"Just fine," I told him.

"You don't sound very fine to me," as he was listening to me breathe. Putting his stethoscope down on his lap, (he had this way of looking right into my eyes), "What's going on?" he asked.

"Nothing but planning a wedding that is out of control," I answered. "I will be okay when it is over."

He pulled out his pad and began to write. He handed me a written prescription and asked me to read it.

Doctor's orders: "Get married one week from Friday."

I looked at him and laughed. "Yeah, right," I said. "I am already in enough trouble for getting engaged Twenty-eight days after meeting this guy."

It was the doctor's turn to laugh. "That's my best advice for your health. Take care of yourself. I will see you in one month."

I still thought it was funny. In fact, I told George and Pat when I got home. I even remember it was on a Wednesday. Thursday, George and Pat told Paul. Paul picked me up at work and said, "We need to talk."

We made a special trip to talk with my parents. Then we had to get by my brother Barry. "Are you sure you know what you are doing," he asked.

We tried to assure him we did.

Barry said, "All right, if you are going to get married this quickly, promise me one thing. If you don't like something that the other person is doing, make it known. It will not get better when you are married."

"Good advice, big brother, good advice."

Paul knew my health issues. We discussed it fully. "It's part of you; I will take it," he said.

I wanted him to be sure about my health issues, and I needed answers as well. We made an appointment to see a geneticist who told us it would be a fifty-fifty chance that we would pass my bone condition on to our children. The more children I had the higher the risk would become. He asked if Paul was from Edinburgh, Scotland, and if so, we shouldn't have any children. This is where my bone condition is prevalent. Paul assured him he was not and that his background was more German than anything else. That was the end of the subject.

I had one week to plan a wedding. I didn't want to just go off and get married. After all, Paul had a church, and doing something like that would not be good for the church or the community.

We planned to have a wedding ceremony on Friday night, but no reception. We would have a best man and maid of honor. I wanted Bonnie, my college roommate, to be my maid of honor. She was planning to come from Ontario in July. There was no way she could come in one week. I asked my sister Marlane to do the honors. She was more than willing to be at my side. She would wear the pink dress that I wore at her wedding as bridesmaid.

I gave up the idea of having flower girls. I had asked Anna-Lise and Sherry and had given them material to make a dress. There was no time, I thought. I thought wrong for their mothers insisted they could have the dresses made in one week.

It was a good thing that my wedding dress was in the process of being made. I wanted a simple white dress. My sister-in-law Geraldine made one, and I loved it.

Marlane went with me to order my flowers. My favorite flower is a white daisy. Even though most brides carry roses, I enjoyed carrying my basket of white daisies with baby's breath.

We all have dreams of what our wedding will be like. I wanted a candlelight service.

For the next two days while at work, I spread the word, "Where can I rent candelabras?"

I pulled out the phone book and called all flower shops. They didn't have any. This was before flower shops rented everything you need for a wedding. I would then ask, "Do you know of any place that may have them?"

They would then give me a phone number and say, "Try here." I tried every number that was given me.

Finally, I got the answer I needed. "Yes, I know who has them."

"Who?" I asked.

"The funeral home."

"Oh, dear," I thought. However, I quickly got passed the squeamish pictures that were passing through my mind. "I need a phone number." And I called it.

After telling a nice gentleman what I was looking for he said, "Yes, we have a pair of candelabras."

I then asked if I could rent them for my wedding on Friday.

He answered, "We have never rented them out before."

"Please, I have been searching for two days."

"I understand," he said, "You can use them for your wedding, but you don't have to rent them. Just pick them up."

Turns out the funeral home was in walking distance of where I worked. We arranged to meet during my lunch hour. I must admit it wasn't the easiest thing for me to open those doors and walk into that funeral home. However, as I did, I told myself to walk straight and not look to the right or to the left. I was aware the funeral home was in business.

What beautiful brass candelabras. They were beautiful, they were big and they were heavy. I could picture them in my wedding. I couldn't picture how I was going to get them back to work and then home on a bus.

The gentleman noticed my concern and he asked me where I lived. When he found out I lived in Fairview a half hour away, he jumped up and clapped his hands.

I jumped two feet.

Love

"This is your lucky day. I have to pick up a body in Fairview this very afternoon. In fact, we could go right now."

"We!" I thought.

"Yes, I can drop you off, but I won't be able to bring you back."

"Good grief!" I thought, and then I heard myself saying, "Let's go."

He carried one candelabra; I carried the other. I followed him out to the hearse, and before I knew it, I was sitting in the front and on my way to Fairview.

Now, George and Pat were eating their lunch, when a hearse drove into the driveway. George had thought he had seen everything, but apparently not, for he could not believe it when I jumped out of that hearse and two candelabras were delivered into his living room.

I had never seen George speechless before, but he was then. I thanked my kind friend and the hearse was on its way.

I looked at George and said, "Please don't ask any questions, but will you drive me back to work?" I don't remember anything that was said on the return to work, and I was only fifteen minutes over my lunch hour.

The next thing I needed was flowers for the church. Where was I going to get flowers for almost no money?

It being March, there were no flowers growing in Nova Scotia, but the Cancer Society was having their annual fund-raising drive. Grocery stores had yellow daffodils to sell. The money went to cancer research.

Even my father brought daffodils home every year in March. I made a trip to the Dominion Grocery Store. Sure enough, there was a new shipment of yellow daffodils. Two big barrels full. I asked for help. The young man asked how many I wanted.

I said, "I want them ALL!!" I must admit, I had a lot of stares at the cash register.

The following Wednesday Paul made an announcement to the people of his church in Mill Village, Shubenacadie. "This is an invitation to my wedding this coming Friday, March 14 at 7 p.m., 48 Convoy Avenue, Fairview." I made the same announcement at my church.

Friday, March 14, at 7 p.m. the church building was packed. The news had reached many people. My father walked me down the aisle of the decorated church to give me away to Paul. I was busy looking to see who was sitting in the pews.

George did the honors of the wedding ceremony. We had a photographer who had just evacuated from Czechoslovakia. He was great, he taught us to all say whisky before he shot the picture because that word makes your eyes open. He took one picture of the whole family and not one had their eyes closed. I requested he not take flash pictures during the ceremony. During the candlelight ceremony, I saw him go into the baptistry door and up the steps to get a picture of the bride and groom standing before George. What this man did not know is there were four feet of water about three feet to his right. It was dark, and I was just waiting to hear a large splash; that would be the end of my photographer. By God's grace, that never happened. My favorite picture of the whole wedding is the shot he took right beside the baptistery.

We had a wonderful wedding. Pat Mansfield stepped in to be Paul's "mother." Afterwards the wedding party and my family celebrated at a local restaurant. We even had a wedding cake. Then we left for a weekend honeymoon.

My heart was at peace. The hurting fire had ended. Just being with Paul was good for my heart. I began to love again.

That was over 36 years ago. It was God's opened door and I have been thankful I had enough faith to walk through.

Several years later, I found out why Bill's parents discarded me. I was not good enough. I had some kind of terrible disease, and their son could certainly find a better wife than I would be.

Not good enough. Cannot measure up, cannot make the goal, falling short, missing the mark and worthless.

Throughout the years, I have heard it said repeatedly. I am not good enough to become a Christian. I will wait until I take care of my problems. I will make everything right, and then I will turn to God. I hate to tell you this, but you will never be good enough. If you are waiting until you are good enough, it will never happen

> "Just as I am, without one plea,
> but that thy blood was shed for me,
> and that thou bidst me come to thee,
> O Lamb of God, I come, I come.
>
> Just as I am, and waiting not
> to rid my soul of one dark blot,
> to thee whose blood can cleanse each spot,
> O Lamb of God, I come, I come.
> with many a conflict, many a doubt,
> fightings and fears within, without,
> O Lamb of God, I come, I come.
>
> Just as I am, poor, wretched, blind;
> sight, riches, healing of the mind,
> yea, all I need in thee to find,
> O Lamb of God, I come, I come.
>
> Just as I am, thou wilt receive,
> wilt welcome, pardon, cleanse, relieve;
> because thy promise I believe,
> O Lamb of God, I come, I come.
>
> Just as I am, thy love unknown
> hath broken every barrier down;
> now, to be thine, yea thine alone,
> O Lamb of God, I come, I come."

This was written by Charlotte Elliott in 1834, and she was right.[13]

Guess what – God wants you when you are not good enough. "Not that we are competent in ourselves to claim anything for ourselves, but our competence comes from God."[14] "God demonstrates his own love for us in this; while we were still sinners, Christ died for us."[15]

You have the wrong concept of God, if you think you have to be perfect before you can have a relationship with Him. The only one perfect was Jesus Christ, God's Son. You are not Jesus Christ. You are not perfect and never will be. We are all sinners. "For all have sinned and fall short of the glory of God."[16]

Remember SIN. Sin separates you from God. It takes a perfect sacrifice to bring you back to God. Where are you going to find someone perfect? Are you perfect? Jesus Christ is perfect.

BINGO.

Jesus Christ can bring you back to God, even when you smell like SIN. Jesus is the perfect sacrifice. He died on the cross for you and me, and He arose the third day. (He did not remain dead). He is a living sacrifice. Moreover, do you know what else? This perfect gift is free. Does not cost you a dime. You do not have to earn brownie points to be good enough. God wants you when you are not perfect. He loves you just the way you are – sin and all.

I am worthy, even if I have funny looking bones on the inside. "Jesus loves me this I know, for the Bible tells me so." And, I believe it.

Love is the best four-letter word in the English language. We can love chocolate, which I do. We can love cats and dogs, which I do. God is love. There is no hate in Him, only love.

I am thankful for the love of God and I am thankful for Paul's love. Thirty-six years ago, I did not know if I could love him enough. It took a long time for my heart to mend completely. However, today, I do not even have a scar, for it has been covered with layers and layers of love from that man from Tennessee sent to me from God.

Love

Dear God:

Thank You for giving me things in this world to love. Those cats brought love to our family. Blake our dog was like a family member. He gave love and joy, and we thank You for these gifts.

However, our children and grandchildren are in a completely different category. Pets are one thing, but these precious children are another. They carry Your spirit, and they look just like You. The love and joy they have brought to Paul and me cannot be measured. Our cup runneth over. Thank You, for they truly are a great gift from You.

And Paul! What can I say about Paul? I prayed to You and asked, "What now?" Your answer was sending me this man from Tennessee. He is kind and loving and would do anything for me. He loves me. I have chosen him as my mate. Help me to be a good wife. Help me to love him as much as he loves me.

Thank you, God, for Paul.
I pray this through Your Son Jesus
Cathy Kenney
 Now
Cathy Wilcoxson

Old Farm House
Mill Village, Shubenacadie, Nova Scotia, Canada

CHAPTER 5 LIFE'S JOURNEY WITH PAUL

I loved being married. Paul and I played house in a small one-bedroom apartment in Milford, Nova Scotia. Just the two of us. I did not notice there was a world around me. It could rain or snow. All I saw was sunshine. The TV news said there were wars and earthquakes. Viet Nam was a terrible war that was still going on. All I knew was Paul.

Like a good new wife, I was cleaning out a closet one morning. Found a box and opened it. There I found award after award. Paul was on the Dean's list so many times at David Lipscomb College that he didn't even open the envelopes. Just tossed them into the box. Congratulations for the top honors for Greek. Honor after honor, and my head began to spin.

What have I done? Paul does not understand. If my mother had received one letter from the Dean, she would have framed it in gold and placed it on the wall for everyone to see. Paul married so beneath him; he married me.

Paul came home for lunch. Instead of finding a sandwich, he found his wife in a heap crying her eyes out. When I told him the problem he said, "Cathy, you scared me half to death. Those honors don't mean nearly as much to me as you do." He held me a long time that day. We did not know each other well. That took place after we were married. We had very interesting times indeed.

Paul preached sermons of Jesus. I taught children about God. Things got even better. We moved to an old farmhouse just down the road from the church building in Mill Village. I was a city girl, but I loved living in the country. We bought groceries in Shubenacadie, the MicMac Indian name for potato. Paul and I loved living in that big farmhouse. We had two black cats Jack and Jill that entertained us. Laundry day was Monday. I hung clothes on a very long clothesline, which was operated by a pulley. To my amazement, people in the village commented that my laundry looked so nice hanging on the clothesline.

Paul and I flew kites and one day the string broke, and we had to chase the kite two farms away before it came back down to the ground. And, of course, that first winter we made two snowmen. They waved at our neighbours for three months.

After the shock of a quick marriage, the community accepted me. It did take ten months. I also had a shock. I woke up one morning and realized I was a preacher's wife. I had no idea how to be a preacher's wife. I hardly knew how to be a wife. I must admit that I loved one lady's comment in Mill Village. She said that I did not act like a preacher's wife, and she thought she and I would be great friends. I took it as a compliment. I do know that Judi MacPhee and I have been friends for more than 35 years.

My sister, Lois, needed a babysitter for Gregory and Ryan, my two nephews. Keith was in Saskatchewan training to become a member of the Royal Canadian Mounted Police. He was graduating and she was to fly out west to be with him. Paul and I volunteered for the job. Ryan was a baby and Gregory was a very active young boy. It was challenging, and I remember one Sunday morning I had both boys ready to go to church. I placed Ryan in his walker and I finished getting myself ready. I heard this awful bang. I ran to see Ryan in the dining room full of dirt from his head to his feet. He had pulled a potted plant down on top of him. He wasn't hurt, but his hair and his eyes and nose were full of dirt. I don't remember how I managed to get him cleaned up and not be late for church.

The babysitting job that was supposed to last a week was extended. It turned out Keith wanted to stop and visit his parents in Ontario. We enjoyed taking care of those boys, but we also decided that we were not yet ready for children of our own.

Those years in Mill Village bring back fond memories. Having Ladies' Days, bringing the residents of a small nursing home to my home for Thanksgiving and the spook house we made in the woodhouse for a Halloween party are just a few memories that I cherish to this day. Not long ago I visited with some of the teenagers that came to that party. They are grown with children of their own. They never forgot that spook house. They were afraid to go through it.

Preacher's wife. Powerful words. I am no longer Cathy; I am the preacher's wife. What comes to your mind when you hear the words preacher's wife? The preacher's wife is different and automatically is separate. Most preachers' wives are strangers to the community; they have no family roots as the rest of the congregation has. Unless the ladies of the congregation rally around her and include her in everything, she remains an outsider. Ladies usually make an effort to do this for the first three years, and after that, the preacher's wife is on her own.

The preacher's wife is known to have all the answers and should be available to all members whenever they need her. They do put her on a pedestal and keep her there until she is needed. Look out if she ever makes a mistake and falls off. Most people have unrealistic expectations of a preacher's wife.

Here I was a preacher's wife. I had just lost my own identity and even my first name. From now on, I would be introduced as the preacher's wife. This is how I will be known the rest of my life. Did you know that some people think that the preacher's wife is public property? If you need anything, just call the preacher's wife.

However, they did not know me. Remember, I am the one who does not let anyone tell me what to do. I was in big trouble.

One congregation where we served, I was in the state of trouble all the time. There was one lady who knew what a preacher's wife was supposed to do, and I wasn't doing it. She would keep a list of my shortcomings, and every three months to the day, she would make a visit to our house. During this time, she would point out, with love, as she put it, all the things I was doing wrong. I could not even remember half of the things that were on her list. This made her even more agitated because I was not taking her seriously. I told her I had a plan. She could be the preacher's wife, but she couldn't have Paul.

What does the scripture say about a preacher's wife? A deacon's wife is to be a "women worthy of respect, not malicious talkers, but temperate and trustworthy in everything."[17] Nowhere in scripture does it say anything about a preacher's wife.

"You are all sons (daughters too) of God through faith in Christ Jesus, for all of you who were baptized into Christ have clothed yourselves with Christ. There is neither Jew or Greek, slave nor free, male nor female, for you are all one in Christ Jesus."[18] It looks to me like we are all to act and behave like a deacon's wife or a preacher's wife. Preacher's wives are no different from any other Christian, and Christians need to be Christ-like. Period.

Being a wife of a doctor does not make you known as a doctor's wife; being a wife of a lawyer does not make you known as a lawyer's wife; being a wife of a meat cutter also does not make you known as a meat cutter's wife. Why should a wife of a preacher be known only as the preacher's wife?

Saying all of this, you may think I do not like being a preacher's wife. But I do! Most of the time that is. I enjoy working with people. I am given the opportunity to teach, serve, help, and love those people who are in need. They are in need of knowing God's Son and what He can do for them. I enjoy seeing lives change for the better when they have Jesus in their lives. I enjoy teaching children about the church of Jesus Christ. How it works, how Jesus is the

Head and we are the body. These children have grown up and are now the leaders in the church today.

I look around at places I have been, and it has amazed me how God has used my life to make a difference for Him in those communities and the lives of people living there. I would not change my life in any way. However, I am a child of God, not just the preacher's wife.

Living with Paul continued to be a great joy. However, all young married couples, including us, have disagreements. Our first argument happened shortly after a snowstorm in March. Paul had these ugly black snow boots that fit over his shoes. It was bad enough he wore them, but he insisted that he tucked his pant legs inside the boots. Knowing Paul is from the South, I explained to him we didn't do that here. It was uncouth. But he said, "I don't understand. Placing your pants on the outside of the boots will make them get wet from the snow."

I assured him he would not be walking through deep snow because it had been shoveled. To no avail, he wasn't budging. One day we were going to the Mall. I told him I wasn't going to get out of the car until he put his pant legs on the outside of his ugly boots. I don't really remember who won (I think I did), but looking back, what a silly thing to argue about.

Just playing house ended for Paul and me. Jennifer was born May 5, 1978. How can you hold your firstborn and not have your heart burst from joy? That little girl stole her daddy's heart right from the beginning. She still holds it to this day. That is okay; God made Paul's heart large enough to love both of his girls.

Three years later, we made the first of our many moves. I did not know then but we began the cycle, preachers come and preachers go. Ontario was the first move. Our son Christopher was born there. Now our family was complete.

Jennifer loved her little brother. She, being five and attending kindergarten, felt very grown up. She took the job of caring for her little brother, Christopher, seriously.

Sometimes she acted too grown up and tried to keep up with her best friend, Aaron. Aaron was a few years older than Jennifer was and was one to try just about anything, at least once. Jennifer, being the tomboy, followed Aaron down dangerous gravel hills on her bike. Of course, she didn't make it, and off to the emergency room, we would go. Doctors removed small stones out of her mouth and nose, and she had a black eye. That was the summer Jennifer was in the emergency room three times. At a church picnic, Aaron found an axe. His sidekick, Jennifer, was right behind him when he raised the axe to cut a piece of wood. Jennifer was hit right between the eyes with the back of the axe. Several stitches and a black eye later, we seriously considered locking her in her bedroom. But the house wasn't safe either. Jennifer decided to give her baby brother his stomach medicine. I walked in just in time to save her brother, but I didn't know if she had taken any, for the bottle was opened and some had spilled out. They pumped her stomach at the emergency room, just to make sure. The last episode happened without Aaron around. She went over her handlebars again while we were camping.

Several days later, we heard a knock at the door. A very nice lady informed me she was from the Family Services Department. She told me that records have shown that my daughter had made several trips to the emergency room, and they wanted to interview me. Of course, I invited her in, but I was embarrassed that they even thought that we would hurt Jennifer. When we moved away from St. Thomas, Jennifer never got hurt again. That's okay, Aaron, we still love you.

Paul was in Canada under the status as missionary. His salary was provided by several churches in Tennessee. After ten years to the day, we were informed that our support would be terminated. Not that Paul did anything wrong; the mission money was being directed to other programs. Prayer again became urgent in knowing which way God wanted us to go.

Paul wanted to go back to school to get a Master's Degree in Counseling. God opened doors and we were moving to Memphis, Tennessee. On the way, we stopped in

Nashville and dropped the children, cats, and dog off at Grandma's house. Paul and I headed for Memphis with the rented truck filled with everything we owned. Finding a hotel, we made two phone calls. One to a real estate company and the other to Walter and Elaine Hart, whom we heard were also in Memphis. Remember Walter Hart? He and Ron Pauls went to talk to my father the night I was baptized.

We bought a small house in one day and then emptied the truck and headed back to Nashville.

Years ago in our early days of marriage, Paul received an inheritance. His grandmother, Erma, left her four grandchildren farm property in Red Hill, Lawrence County, Tennessee. The farm consisted of 80 acres and was known for its very fertile soil. For several generations, cotton and soybeans were harvested there. For a few years, Paul's younger brother, Robert, tried to farm the land. It wasn't long before everyone had moved away. The decision was made to sell the property, and the money was divided amongst the four children. We put the money down on our first house in Mill Village. We never touched the money except to buy houses. Several places we lived in houses belonging to the church. We did buy our own house in Mill Village, Pittsburgh and now in Memphis.

This was December. We were settled again, and Paul started classes at the Harding Graduate School in January.

How were we going to live? We had no jobs. God would provide we thought, and He did. It turned out the Graduate School was looking for a secretary. I applied for the job. I remember the interview well. Dr. Hazelip, the Dean, and I had a very good visit. I told him everything I could do and he said I had the job. Later I found out they did not usually hire student wives for faculty secretaries, but they made an exception in my case. God kept opening doors and I kept going through.

Here I go again. What have I done? This girl from Nova Scotia just convinced a dean of a graduate school, she could take care of six professors. I was scared to death. I called on God and He was there. I believe God was preparing me. Why else would I be among some of the best teachers of God's word? I was secretary to Dr. Philip Slate, Dr. Rick Oster, Dr. Earl West, and Dr. W.B. West and had association with many more professors.

Not only was Paul a full-time student, he took any part-time job he could get. There were many: a bellhop, post office, copying medical records, cleaning bookstores, and Federal Express. Here I was a working mother, something I never wanted to do. I thought, "Only we can take care of our children." Now what? We all have to do things we do not like to do. Never say "never". We just have to get over it. Daycare now became a part of the Wilcoxson family.

Daycare. What goes through your mind when you think of Daycare? A beautiful place where lines of children walk through the hallways, making their way to exciting classes developed just for their age group? Children of all ages smiling and happy to be there, while their parents are working? An outdoor playground where the children get along with one another, with many teachers watching over their cluster of little ones? This type of Daycare does exist, but costs lots of money. We did not have money. We depended upon the wives of students who had small children of their own and were trying to make money to keep their husbands in school. My child did not get the first priority, not even the second, or third, and maybe not even the fourth in line for attention.

I remember well the day that the Challenger exploded during liftoff on January 28, 1986. Unfortunately, so does my son, for when he was two years old the babysitter let him watch the spacecraft blow up repeatedly that day on TV. For a very long time, whenever my son saw an airplane he asked if it was going to blow up. We also had the children in a public daycare centre for the summer. Today they are grown and can still tell me stories of that place.

Children are a lot tougher than parents think. My children were no exception. It is actually harder for the parents than for their children. It did not mean that Paul and I would have to like it. For that reason, as soon as one of us was off work, or school ended, the children were picked up and brought home whether daycare was ended or not. The daycare people never did understand.

I wish my children did not have memories of daycare. My memories – they were lost. My son was age two at the time. I do not have the same memories I did of his sister at the same age. Someone else was there to see him play. Someone else was there to fix his lunch. Someone else placed the Band-Aid on his skinned knee.

Do not think I am naive enough to think that daycare is not necessary, for in this imperfect world it is very necessary. Most families need help giving the basic needs to their young children. Most parents have to work to make money to support their families. I just wish it were not so. Nevertheless, I do know one thing; God has a special place in His heart for children. Jesus said, "Let the little children come to me, and do not hinder them, for the kingdom of heaven belongs to such as these." [19]

I have a warning here. If anyone hurts a little child on purpose in any way, that person will have to stand before God one day. That person will not be very happy. You know what I am talking about.

Hard Times. We all have them. I guarantee that sometime in your life you will experience hard times. I do not even have to explain the meaning; you already know. Hard times are what you make of them. Paul and I learned many lessons during these years. One was that we had to accept help. We have always been on the helping end. Now we needed to be on the receiving end. It is easier to give than to receive. The church and our dear sisters and brothers reached out to us, and our needs were met. From that time on, we could help others, knowing how much it feels to hurting people.

Christmas time came and we had no money. We did not care about us, but the children needed Santa to visit. Christmas presents that year were homemade. Paul took Jennifer to a woodworking shop to make me three wooden geese. They painted them and put ribbons around their necks. I believe they were one of the best presents I have ever received. Uncle Russell always sent money at Christmas and we used it as such. The church gave us a basket full of goodies. The children did not know we were having difficulties that year; we did not want them to know. Let them be children. Do not put the world's problems on your young children's shoulders. We could have cried, "Woe is me," and felt sorry for ourselves. We are happy; we love God whether in lean times or times of plenty. You will have both in this life; how will you react to them?

Race. What does it mean? I am not talking about running a race. Race seems to be divided into categories. Red, white, black and a lot in between. When I was a baby, my mother sang a song while rocking me in a rocking chair. The song was handed down three generations. We called it "Stay in Your Own Backyard."

******

> Lilac trees are bloomin' in the garden by
> the fence
> Mammy's at her little cabin door
> Curly headed picanniny comin' home
> from school
> Cryin' cuz his little heart is sore
>
> All the children play around
> With skins so white and fair
> None of them with him would ever play
> So mammy in her lap, took that
> weeping little chap
> And sang in her own kind way
>
> Why don't you play in your own backyard
> Never mind what the white chile say
> What do you suppose they're going to give
> A black little coon like you
>
> Go out and play as long as you please
> But Honey don't you cry so hard

> Go out and jump on the high board fence
> But stay in your own backyard[20]

This song taught me when I was very young not to be prejudiced. Living in Nova Scotia gave me a limited association with Black people. Nova Scotia has the highest population of Blacks in Canada. Even with my limited association, I could tell they were not treated fairly.

Back when I was at Great Lakes Christian College, the chorus made a trip to Buffalo, New York. We sang at a Black congregation. They showed us such a good time, and I was fascinated. My roommate, Bonnie, and I stayed at Sister Young's, who had college age sons. When the sons picked us up to go to their house, I will never forget what they asked of us. "Would you please hide yourselves in the back seat? It would not be good for the police to see we have two young White girls with us."

When we arrived at their home, their mother welcomed us with a gift and later on in the evening a warning. "Don't go outside. It is not safe." All through the night, we heard police sirens and even people running through the alleyway. We had a story to tell the next day when we joined the rest of the group. They had stories to tell too.

Two years later when I had returned from Ontario to Nova Scotia, I made a trip to Texas with a group who had come to teach VBS. I found out that we were going to stay at the same congregation while traveling. What was very interesting was that I was the only one who knew it was a Black congregation. I thought it would be better to tell them before we arrived. I took the leader aside and broke the news. He did not believe me, for if it were a Black congregation, he would know it. I assured him it was and told him the address, the preacher's name and directions to get there. His eyes got rather large, and I could see he was troubled indeed. I knew there were several on that bus who would not be happy. I offered my assistance to prepare those in our group for an experience of a lifetime. I believe God used me to prevent a bad situation from happening to loving black Christian people, who were willing to open their doors to strangers and show the love of God. This group too had many stories to tell the next day. This was the second time I stayed with Sister Young. What a blessing from God.

A few months before Paul graduated from Harding Graduate School, we put out the word that we would be looking for a church. Many weekends we traveled. We traveled all over Mississippi and Tennessee. It did not matter where we went; we were letting God lead. We were looking for His open doors and if not a door a window. The times we traveled by car the children went with us. However, when we had to fly, we left our children with

Annie and Ronnie Young. Our house became their house for the weekend. The neighbours were not happy, nor did they understand why we would let a Black couple take over our house, even if they were taking care of our children. We all loved Annie and Ronnie, especially our children. I thank God our children could experience the love shown by this wonderful couple.

Paul and I have been blessed to work with our Black brothers and sisters on many occasions and in many places. In Pittsburgh, I spoke at a "Ladies' Day." The only White ladies were the ones that came with me. In Louisiana and California, I spoke for Black congregations. One of the most fun memories Paul and I have is teaching a VBS teen class in Louisiana. We had thirty-five teenage kids or more crowded into a small room (without air conditioning). We had a lively class, to say the least. Two men came to check us out to see if everything was going all right. He found two teachers laughing along with a room full of kids. We were the only white people in the building.

Let me tell you one more story. Christopher our son was one of the top students in high school in DeQuincy, Louisiana. The last part of his senior year, he was looking for scholarships to attend college. He applied for all of them. One was to the AKA Sorority at McNeese State University in Lake Charles, Louisiana. It was a group of Black ladies. He was invited to come speak to them. Not very many white students applied. Christopher had no problem going among this group. They asked him one question. "If you could have lunch with any person in the world, either someone in the present or someone in history, who would it be?"

Without hesitation, he replied, "That is easy, Jesus Christ, and let me tell you why."

As we walked into our house, returning from the interview, the phone was ringing. Christopher got the scholarship. We were told that most white students who tried for this scholarship always answered, "Martin Luther King," or some other famous black person. They thought that Christopher's answer came genuinely from his heart. It did not matter what colour they were or what he was.

That is how it is with God. It does not matter what colour you are.

"The God who made the world and everything in it is the Lord of heaven and earth and does not live in temples built by hands. And he is not served by human hands, as if he needed anything, because he himself gives ALL men life and breath and everything else. From one man he made every nation of men, that they should inhabit the whole earth; and he determined the times set for them and the exact places where they should live. God did this so that men would seek him and perhaps reach out for him and find him, though he is not far from each ONE of us. For in him we live and move and have our being. As some of your own poets have said, 'We are his offspring'."[21]

God is interested in your heart. Give your heart, give your life, and give your soul back to Him.

As Paul and I live this journey, we try to stop and figure out what we are really doing. Are we still looking for those open doors? Are we working so hard for God that we do not see Him guide us? People have said to stop and smell the roses. Do we stop and continue to give our hearts to the One who really wants them? Let us not forget whom we are doing the great deeds for. Let us stop and renew every morning, give your heart, give your life, give your soul back to God. Oh, yes and your life will get even better.

Life's Journey with Paul

Dear God,

Thank You, God, for the children I teach here in Mill Village. Help me to teach them about You and Your Son Jesus. Help me teach them that Jesus loves them.

Be with Paul as he shares the Gospel with neighbours and friends. Let them have open hearts.

Help me to be a preacher's wife. I am now expected to play a new role in my life. However, I do not know the script. Help me to learn. But most of all, help me to learn what You want of my life.

We received Your gift on May 5th. A baby girl. How did You know my heart was asking for a daughter. But then I forget, You know everything. Thank You for Jennifer Catherine Anne.

Your second gift arrived four and a half years later. A son! Christopher Paul Edward. I could not dare hope for a boy. I thought I was asking too much. I thought two girls would have been fine to fill my heart. A Son! You gave me a man-child. My heart was filled with great joy.

Paul is a fine father. He teaches them about You. Help us both be good parents.

Thank you again for our daughter and son.
This prayer is prayed in Your Son's name.
Cathy Wilcoxson

Our House in Baldwin Borough, Pittsburgh, Pennsylvania

CHAPTER 6 WHAT ARE ROOTS?

Moving was not so bad. I am a girl who had been raised in Nova Scotia and had not been a hundred miles away from home until the age of fourteen. I lived in Ontario twice; Memphis, Tennessee, and now I was headed for Pittsburgh, Pennsylvania. The longest roots we ever put down were here in Pittsburgh for nine years. Ask my children where they are from, and they consider Pittsburgh their home. We watched them grow from children to teenagers.

The Wilcoxsons enjoyed living in their own home in Pittsburgh. We bought a house on top of a hill. There is nothing but hills in Pittsburgh, and I didn't want to live on the bottom but on the top of a hill.

I have fond memories living in Pittsburgh. I loved the church and her people. I enjoyed every moment of watching our children grow while they were in grade school. Jennifer was into softball and chorus. Christopher was into music and marching bands. This was the most exciting time of our lives. For nine years, everything went fine. I even told Paul not to talk too loud about his children. I didn't want Satan to take notice and come after us again.

My mother came to visit more than once. In addition, Russell and Grandma came to see us. They both came for Jennifer's graduation from high school. I got comfortable in Pittsburgh. Too comfortable, and I forgot what happens when God is put on the back burner.

The day was May 5, Jennifer's eighteenth birthday. There was a knock at the door. Bill was standing on our porch; he brought some unwelcome news. Today the church voted whether we should stay or go. Bill brought the bad news in person. We asked God for mercy and strength.

How did the children react to the vote? Christopher started packing that very afternoon. Jennifer got mad and said it did not affect her because she was going away to college anyway.

After checking and rechecking different churches all summer, we thought we had found a church in Virginia. Christopher, Paul and I had a wonderful weekend visiting

What Are Roots?

them. They seemed to be very interested and told us not to move to any other church before they could get back to us. We went back to Pittsburgh happy and waiting for a phone call, a phone call that never came. We received a letter in the mail that said they had accepted someone else. It was hard on all of us, especially Christopher. What had happened?

The search continued and we decided we would go to Cumberland, Maryland. We did pray constantly about this move. However, looking back, we really did not ask. I think that we just told God we would go there. I don't think we had recovered from the rejection we had just experienced. I had forgotten how it felt to see God open doors.

What had changed? Me. I had. I thought I was a good Christian. I went through all the motions. But it was all about me. I did not want to leave Pittsburgh. I had forgotten preachers come and preachers go. Just like the change of season. But, why? Why did we have to leave?

It did not matter why; it was going to happen. Paul and I were going to be tested.

Tested. The act of undergoing testing, example; he survived the greatest test of battle. Trial – Something that tests a person's endurance of forbearance."

I never liked tests. In school, if a test were placed in front of me, I would freeze. All throughout my life, I had to take tests. Moving as many times as we have, I have taken drivers tests in six states and two provinces of Canada. Each one was hard for me. I took a test in San Diego, California to become a citizen of the United States of America. I have taken tests for jobs, such as the Census Board in Indiana. I would take weeks to prepare.

Did you know that if you are a follower of God, you are going to be tested? I guarantee it. My tests came in the form of preachers come and preachers go. After living in Pittsburgh, I found out I did not like moving. Satan found my Achilles Heel.

What is your Achilles Heel? I am sure Satan has discovered it by now. He is good at that. Do you remember when I was a new Christian that I said, "Satan, bring it on? It does not matter what you do to me. I will continue to serve this God I had found."

Life has passed by since then. I forgot to lean on God at least as much as I did when I first met Him. We are tested; it comes in cycles. When we get too comfortable.

". . . who through faith are shielded by God's power until the coming of the salvation that is ready to be revealed in the last time. In this you greatly rejoice, though now for a little while you may have had to suffer grief in all kinds of trials. These have come so that your

What Are Roots?

faith – may be proved genuine and may result in praise, glory and honor when Jesus Christ is revealed."[22]

Moving to Cumberland, Maryland was difficult. We had not sold our house in Pittsburgh yet. A mortgage payment plus rent was overbearing. A decision was made to live in our small travel trailer, right on the church property. Christopher told his friends at school that he lived close to the Church of Christ church building on the corner of East Fourth St. and Memorial Avenue.

Paul and I did not move to Cumberland for the right reason. We were in a hurry to get Christopher settled in high school and did not wait for God to open the door; we opened it for Him. Satan was happy; he made our lives miserable. Crying out to God, we said, "We can serve you anywhere; we will stay here." To make a long story short, we found leaders who were not godly men. They asked us to leave less than a year later. Paul and I were told to have everything we owned out of the church building in three days.

"Okay, God, now what do we do? Is the test over yet? I hope so, but I know you will take care of us. God, we will go anywhere North. Show us the way."

Do you think when you are tested it only affects you? Satan does not work that way. It affects everyone around you, especially your family. Several years later Christopher wrote this:

The Year Our World Turned Upside-down: According to Me

Faith is something everyone has. However, not everyone uses it correctly. Faith is a seed that God planted inside of us. He intended that seed to grow into a large, blooming flower that becomes who we are. In order for faith to grow, it must be stretched, battered, and treated in a way that it should not. I have learned from past experiences what faith really is. In the year of late 1996 to early 1997, my faith, along with my family's, was tested in no way I could ever imagine. I knew life would be hard, filled with hard times and sorrows, but nothing could prepare me for the year my world turned upside-down.

Paul Wilcoxson, my father, is a preacher and has been for several years. Before this, however, he was a missionary in Nova Scotia, Canada. This is where he met my mother,

What Are Roots?

Catherine, where they fell in love and were married. Yes, my mother married the missionary. It has been a joke at many dinner tables across the continent. They stayed in Nova Scotia for three or four years, where they had my older sister, Jennifer. In 1982, they moved to St. Thomas, Ontario, just enough time to give birth to me. In 1984, we all moved to Memphis, TN, where my dad went back to school to get his Masters degree. Completing his schooling, we began searching for a place to work. In 1987, my dad started preaching at the Whitehall Church of Christ in Pittsburgh, PA. This is the place I grew up in. From the age of four up to ninth grade, I lived happily in a small borough several miles from the downtown area. I grew up in a Christian environment where I hardly knew any hardships. I was baptized when I was thirteen, and I lived as good ofaChristian life as I could.

May 5, 1996, we received the confirming phone call that we were out of a job. What a birthday present for my sister. We had been talking about it for weeks before this day, but I still was not prepared for the shock. I could not understand why the church that had loved us for nine years wanted to get rid of us. We did not do anything wrong. I did not realize how hard it would be to pull out our roots that we had grown and drag them somewhere else. I did not want to leave all my friends behind. I had too many.

The long search began. Most people do not understand how hard it is to find a church that needs a preacher, and what their families have to go through in order to find one. My dad began making sermon tapes and filling out resumes and sending them to several churches. We got some bites, but it was still a hard struggle. Finally, our prayers were answered by a church in northern Virginia. We went to the town for the weekend and preached and fellowshipped with the members there. They made us feel welcome. I even participated in a childcare camp and got to know a lot of the teens there. We went home on Monday feeling good

What Are Roots?

that we had found a church that liked us and we liked them. A weekend later, we got a call from them telling us that they had found someone else. Heartbroken, I cried to God asking Him why this was happening to us.

    A few weeks later, another phone call asked us to come to a small town in western Maryland called Cumberland. Cumberland is a small railroad town. Most of the people are friendly. There is one McDonald's in town, the rest of the restaurants are a few miles down the interstate along with a small mall and movie theater. The town is located in the valley of four mountains. The weather there is wonderful because the mountains broke off most of the rain and storms. The worst weather they ever get is cloudy days! There is a train engineer school in downtown Cumberland. This brings in most of the business. There are two rivalry schools: Fort Hill High and Allegheny High. Sounds like a perfect, little town, right? My parents and I drove the three-hour trip, not really anticipating the try-out. After the last trip, it just was not exciting anymore. We arrived in Cumberland and were greeted by a very friendly man. He took us out to eat and brought us to a nice hotel. My dad preached there on Sunday. By the way, usually, preachers that try-out at different churches use the same sermon over and over again. To me, it was not interesting after the tenth time. The church there loved the sermon. Right then and there, they offered my dad the job. We stayed overnight again for two days contemplating the job. We accepted the position and right before school started for that year, we moved to Cumberland.

It was traumatic for me, leaving all my friends behind. I did not know how to break the news to them that I was leaving the town I had grown up in. I waited until the last minute so I would not have to live with the sadness too long. Although, I think it would have been easier on me to tell them right away instead of holding it all in and living life like normal. After the move, I did not keep in touch. I lost their addresses and phone numbers in the move. I have no idea *how they are doing or if they even think of me. All I have are a bunch of memories and a shoebox filled with pictures. I found new friends, and actually, they have been the greatest circle of friends I have ever had. We planted our roots one last time, hoping for a new, thriving relationship with our new church. I did not know it then, but I know it now that the seed that God planted in me was growing. It was preparing me for what evils would lie ahead in life. Moreover, bad times are what make us who we are. As an eighth grader, I could not understand this, but I do now. Troubles bring sorrow; sorrows bring strength; strength brings faith; and faith brings maturity, love, and happiness.*

For parents to hear from the heart of one's son can be heartbreaking. I am proud of my son, for his faith in God is strong. The experience Christopher had in Cumberland, Maryland almost cost him his faith in God. We knew it was bad and to protect our son we sent him back to Pittsburgh. We sent him to church camp, Camp Concern for three weeks. The wonderful teachers there and our good friends helped Christopher save his faith in his God.

Life at times can seem unfair, but God did not promise us a life without troubles. He promised us a life where He would be beside us.

This was the time of life when I decided I did not like moving. However, God wasn't finished preparing me for what He wanted of me. Since then, we have moved nine times and counting. Three of those were testing. Six were healing and serving the Lord with wonderful Christian people.

There is a good side to all this moving around. Do you know how many friends we have? More than we can count. I have always told people I would keep in touch at least once a year. My Christmas card list is huge. God has blessed us with wonderful friends. Without them, we would never have made this journey with God.

It didn't work out for us in Cumberland. In retrospect, there were several "red flags" about Cumberland that we should have heeded. In addition, the fact that Paul's heart wasn't in the decision, to begin with, should have been a telltale sign. Had Paul only listened to his heart, perhaps some of the hardships endured might have been avoided.

Looking back, we should have retreated from Cumberland as soon as we arrived due to the way we were

What Are Roots?

treated about the salary issue. We had only been in Cumberland a few hours, and because Paul did not preach that Sunday morning, they didn't want to pay him a full week's salary without taking a vacation day. Paul did not tell me this until several months later. I believe he was embarrassed. Treating a preacher that way the first day he arrived was without excuse.

It was a relief when we were free to look for another congregation. We were determined to listen to God this time. We didn't want to make another mistake.

God has a sense of humor. We asked to go anywhere north. God opened the door and He sent us south, DeQuincy, Louisiana, a place to heal, until Satan decides to test again. You know it is coming.

*****

So what are roots? My daughter Jennifer has been married 13 years. Except for one year, she has lived in the same town. She has more roots than I have.

People have said, "How can you do it? Leaving your children behind; I just couldn't."

You think it is easy for me? God did not say it would be easy. I am not the only grandmother who lives far away from three wonderful grandsons. I think that I will start a club. I will call it 'Those of us who can't hug our grandchildren'. If you are blessed to live near your family, be thankful. Be kind and helpful to us that are not.

Then there are other people that say, "I wish I were you. I have lived in the same town since I was born." It is funny – those who have roots wish they did not, and those who do not have roots wish they did. That is why one of my favourite scriptures is "Not that I speak from want, for I have learned to be content in whatever circumstances I am."[23]

When Paul moved me out of Nova Scotia and away from my family, he made a promise that he has tried to keep. The promise was to bring me home to visit every two or three years, no matter what. I have not kept count, but I believe he has held to that promise very well. Times when I was homesick I would say, "Take me home for a visit and I will be ready to go for another year or two." We have a joke in the family. Do not let mother watch Anne of Green Gables movies. For Anne and I have much in common. She spent her summers in a small community by the ocean and her favorite place to go was the lighthouse. I spent my summers in Sheet Harbour by the ocean and my grandparents were lighthouse keepers. My favourite thing to do was run across the field towards the lighthouse.

This girl from Nova Scotia, has she forgotten her roots? I never can.

What Are Roots?

Do I have new roots? Yes, short and strong. God has opened doors for me, and yes, windows as well. I have been blessed to experience many cultures and many ways of living. Such places as the beautiful hills of Pennsylvania, the semi-tropical climate of Louisiana, the beauty and fair weather of California and the fields and fields of growing corn in Indiana. They all fascinate me. However, I have two long roots. Roots that are strong in the love I have for my God. In addition, the deep, loving roots Paul and I share. I think Paul loves me more than I love him, if that could even be possible.

What Are Roots?

Dear God,

Every time we move, I think of it as a great adventure for You, God. Meeting new Christians and being invited to work among them, to take the Gospel throughout this land is a privilege.

My roots were trying to grow deeper. The moving became a burden for me. It hurt for my roots to be torn up and put into a moving truck to start all over again. Why can't we just teach people about You and Your Son where we are?

Moving from Canada was both hard and exciting all at the same time. I told You many years ago, I will go anywhere You wanted me to go. I wish You wouldn't hold me to it as often as You do.

God, I guess You noticed I changed my name. If I were moving to the USA, then I would change my name back to what it was when I was born. Catherine. I was named after my grandmother. I prefer it to Cathy. Therefore, I introduced myself to all the new people as Catherine. I have been known as Catherine for over 25 years now.

Leaving Pittsburgh was even harder than leaving Canada.

I DID NOT WANT TO LEAVE. However, You had other plans and told me to get over it. First, You would teach me a lesson.

I know, God, I deserved the lesson. We were not even waiting for You to open doors. We were opening them ourselves and slamming them behind us right in Your face.

FORGIVE ME, LORD. I learned Your lesson well. Then You opened a door that gave us a time of healing. For that, I am grateful. However, six years later, I had to learn the same lesson all over again. I did not want to leave Louisiana. Sorry, I am so slow to learn.

Help me to let You steer my life. Let me be happy for where I am. Let me talk with You. You will show me the way. Then I will be happy.

I pray this to You, God.

Catherine Wilcoxson

Open Doors and Open Windows: Journey with God

CHAPTER 7 GOD-GIVEN TALENTS - YOURS AND MINE

Talent. A natural aptitude or skill. A natural ability, a gift. A person who possesses unusual ability in some field or activity. Expert."

Growing up as children, we develop talents by our environment. Being from a large family, who required you to gather at the dinner table once a day, gave time to learn all kinds of different talents. This mealtime was a time of sharing each other's day. Everyone participated whether you were in grade school or a university student. There were always both at our table. My father sat at the end of the table in our dining room. My mother to the left of him. And, more often than not, a baby in a highchair between them. The rest of us kids had our places to sit. I can close my eyes and see my brothers and sisters sitting at their places at the table. There was no fighting or fussing; my father did not allow it. I learned a lot from that fellowship.

The first thing I learned was to cook. My mother was a cook in the Navy in World War II; we ate well. Cooking for eight just came naturally. To this day, I love to have large groups of people into our home to share great food and great company.

Today very few families sit down at a table and eat a meal together. They sit in front of the TV or eat standing up at the kitchen counter. They are very busy people. The whole family, children and adults, have their own separate activities. They are all going in different directions, and it takes a lot of energy to get everyone to the place they need to go. Are you using the same degree of energy to make sure your family knows God?

Have you ever disturbed an ant hill? In Louisiana, there are fire ants, and you had better know if you have disturbed their nest. You will not know the ants are on you until it is too late, for they wait until several are on you, and then they give some kind of signal to bite all at the same time. Their bites feel like fire. Millions of ants are running everywhere. They seem to be running in every direction at the same time. I wonder if God looks down and sees His children acting just like those ants, running in every direction. The problem is God never gets to know the children who are running here and there and everywhere.

> "Be still, and know that I am God; I will be exalted among the nations, I will be exalted in the earth." [24]

Of course, education is the clearest ways to develop talents. The school days of our lives are the years we are carefree to experiment with what we are good at. I thank God I found Him during those years. Great Lakes Christian College was the beginning of training for me to serve people for the rest of my life. It was directly after GLCC I began using talents to support myself. I knew office skills and that is how I found my first job at Dalhousie University in Halifax, Nova Scotia. I used the same talents in Memphis while working at Harding Graduate School of Religion. I have fallen back on those skills or talents throughout my life. In addition, I have learned that I have many more talents to use for the service of God.

What is a talent? In scripture, we read many lessons on talents.

> "Again, it will be like a man going on a journey, who called his servants and entrusted his property to them. To one he gave five talents of money, to another two talents, and

to another one talent, each according to his ability. Then he went on his journey.

The man who had received the five talents went at once and put his money to work and gained five more.

So also, the one with the two talents gained two more. But the man who had received the one talent went off, dug a hole in the ground and hid his master's money.

"After a long time the master of those servants returned and settled accounts with them.

The man who had received the five talents brought the other five. 'Master,' he said, 'you entrusted me with five talents. See, I have gained five more.'

"His master replied, 'Well done, good and faithful servant! You have been faithful with a few things; I will put you in charge of many things. Come and share your master's happiness!'

"The man with the two talents also came. 'Master,' he said, 'you entrusted me with two talents; see, I have gained two more.'

"His master replied, 'Well done, good and faithful servant! You have been faithful with a few things; I will put you in charge of many things. Come and share your master's happiness!'

"Then the man who had received the one talent came. 'Master,' he said, 'I knew that you are a hard man, harvesting where you have not sown and gathering where you have not scattered seed.

So I was afraid and went out and hid your talent in the ground. See, here is what belongs to you.'

"His master replied, 'You wicked, lazy servant! So you knew that I harvest where I have not sown and gather where I have not scattered seed?

Well then, you should have put my money on deposit with the bankers, so that when I returned I would have received it back with interest.

"'Take the talent from him and give it to the one who has the ten talents.

For everyone who has will be given more, and he will have an abundance. Whoever does not have, even what he has will be taken from him.

And throw that worthless servant outside, into the darkness, where there will be weeping and gnashing of teeth.'"[25]

Whatever talents you have, God expects you to use them with confidence for Him.

1. Have you ever sat down and made a list of your talents? It may surprise you how long your list becomes. What are my talents? The list may go like this.
2. Teacher. I love to teach. Children, teenagers, and adults.
3. Organizer. I can organize anything. Vacation Bible Schools, Summer Day Camps, and Fall Festivals. Honorary dinners for the police, firefighters, teachers, city workers. Parenting classes, daycare and nursery classes.
4. I can write. Church bulletins, class material, letters, and books.
5. I can work with the elderly; comfort the grieving, plan funerals and funeral dinners.
6. I can encourage. Expecting mother, young mothers with new babies, advice for the terrible 'twos', holding your hand when dealing with teenagers.
7. I can grow flowers and tomatoes. Both I share with everyone around me.

8. I love to decorate my house and enjoy a clean environment to live in.
9. I continue to learn to sew, make quilts and try to craft.

How is your list coming? Have I got you started? Your list can go on and on. My list continues to grow. I have done all these things in the work of the Lord, standing beside my husband. We have always worked as a team. He has encouraged me; I have encouraged him. God has encouraged us both. Many times I have heard it said, "You get two for one when you hire Paul as a preacher."

God has helped me grow into the talents that I have today. God opened doors and windows and I always went through. I take that back; I always tried to go through; however, many times, I was afraid, but one thing I always knew, God was with me when I stepped out of my comfort zone. I had God on one side of me and Paul on the other. Without the two, I would never have been able to grow in my talents.

Looking back on my life, I have followed my mate to six states and two provinces of Canada to work in God's kingdom. We have raised two children and are now enjoying four grandchildren. I have given the work of my talents freely; very seldom did I charge money for my labors. This may have been good to many, but it may have hurt me in my old age. I did not collect points for social insurance and social security, making retirement income sparse at the least.

Money. We all need it, some of us love it, and we all seem to want more. I have had no great desire for money. Every time we have extra, we seem to give it away. Paul is a lucky man to have such a low maintenance woman. The desire to shop hits me once a year at Christmas, for I love to buy for others. I have no desire to buy for myself. Paul and I can get by with very little money. That is one reason we have chosen to work with small churches of the Lord. We have received everything we have needed and wanted. God has blessed us, as we work and form relationships with people in smaller groups. The work has always been challenging and has kept our lives very interesting. We wake up every day not sure of what the day will bring. However, that keeps our lives interesting and we never have time to be bored. When we change from full-time church work to part time work, we will continue to find ways to have money come in. God will be beside us, as He always has been.

Do I have second thoughts about the way we chose to use and make money? Sometimes, usually when I see how other people use money so freely. Maybe they do things that we would not even think of doing. There was a time I had access to money. I have close friends who do have money. They soon found out I would have loved them whether they had money or not. Maybe that is why I had opportunities to help people using my friend's money. I was given a credit card, and when I saw someone in need, I would make sure his or her needs were taken care of. I must admit, I remember trips I went on with these generous people who would give me money to spend. There was one condition; I had to spend the money on myself during the trip. I could not take any home. They knew me well.

Learn to use your money well. It is a gift from God. Be very careful of credit cards; they can ruin your life. Credit cards are good when they are used as a tool for organizing the money you have coming in. However, when this tool becomes a monster and has rule over you, then you may need to look behind you and see who is laughing at you. Satan himself.

Like everyone else, we try to live with the income God has blessed us with. However, there are times when there is not enough money. We have all been there. Medical bills may hang over your head; mortgage payments, car payments, food bills are only the beginning. We have the heavy burden of learning the talent to master the system here on earth, but thank God, we will not need money in heaven.

How do you know what your talents are?

God is not going to have an apple drop on your head to let you know the answer. You will also never know sitting around doing nothing. Many sit around and say they do not know what their talents are. They keep blinders on, and until they take them off, they will never know what their talents are.

Blinders were used for horses. The horse was tricked to look straight ahead. That kept them out of trouble; they could not look right or left. If you have blinders on, you may get to the end of your destination by looking only straight ahead; but think of what you have missed along the way. You did not see the beautiful flowers, green meadows, tall mountains, blue skies. You did not see frogs, and birds, deer or skunks. You did not see the wonders of children, the elderly and teachers. You did not see those who were hurting, those in need, and those who need your help. Take your blinders off and you will see your talents. Do not be afraid to try new things, go to new places and to explore the world God has given to us. When you step out and do new things, you will find talents you never knew you possessed. You may see a talent that God wanted you to see a long time ago. You may stumble upon a talent you would not have dreamed you could or would ever do.

Look at me. I did not know I could write until I was in my 50's. It has changed my life. God has blessed me because I stepped out into a brand new world, a world of writing.

My writing started when my mother was 80 years old. She was spending the winter with me in Louisiana. Have you ever heard someone say," I wished I had asked my grandmother that question?" However, it was too late because that grandmother was now gone. I was not going to let that happen to me. I sat my mother down for one morning a week and interviewed her. I began with the question, "What do you remember about your grandparents?" I ended with several printed copies of my mother's life that I gave for Christmas presents to the family. Halfway through this project, I found out I could write and liked doing so.

God has opened so many doors because of my book, *"The Adventures of Captain Heman Kenney and Lady Catherine 1833-1917."* I know you would enjoy reading it, so check out the website www.theladycatherinecompany.com. It will give you information on how to order that book. I have been able to share my faith that I have in my God. The God I found back in my teen years. I can tell people that God really loves me and His Son Jesus really saved my soul.

What other talents do I have? I do not know. But I do know that God is not finished with me yet. For all the years I have left to walk this earth will be ones following in the footsteps of Jesus, which will direct me face to face with my God.

God-Given Talents – Yours and Mine

Dear God,

You are a wonderful, God, and I know you care for me and watch over me. Keep me safe from Satan.

Thank You for my talents. Help me use them in Your kingdom. Thank you for allowing me to find new ones. The ones You pushed me into. Thank You for pushing.

Thank you for fire ants. I am not sure why You made them. However, You know far more than I do. Help us not to act like them, running around in all directions, hurting people. Help us to love one another.

Thank You for loving me.

In Jesus name,

Catherine Wilcoxson

Open Doors and Open Windows: Journey with God

**Baptistery
Orchard Hills Church
Covington, Indiana**

CHAPTER 8 BAPTISM

I have fond memories as a child of family getting together for a very special occasion. A christening of a baby.

The whole family was standing at the front of a beautiful church. Stain glass windows picturing the Gospel of Christ surrounding us. A candle in a red glass container hanging over the baptismal font. (I must admit the font looked to me like a very large birdbath. But no birds for that day.) My father stood straight like a statue, dressed in his only suit. Wearing a white starched shirt and dark tie and black shoes that were shined. He had taken his place by my mother who was already standing around the baptismal font. I always thought my mother was the most beautiful woman that I had ever seen. This day I felt no different, for she was beautiful standing there in her skirt and jacket that she had made. She always wore heels and red lipstick. Here she was today standing there holding a baby, the last of her sons.

The baby was the limelight of the occasion, for it was for him we were there. He had his white christening clothes on. A white gown that almost hung to the knees of my mother. A white bonnet and matching booties with white ribbons that were tied in bows. His large dark eyes were open and he was looking around. I do not think he noticed the minister standing there in his white robe. He also had strips of gold silk that were embroidered and a small cross hanging around his neck. Nor did he notice the godparents, who witnessed and took an oath that they would see this child raised knowing God.

My mother untied the bow of his bonnet, which was slipped off, revealing a small head full of dark hair. The ceremony began with the minister taking the baby and carefully holding him over the font. Reading from his book, which was on a stand, he raised his free arm up and made the sign of the cross in the air. He then took the clamshell, scooped up holy water from the font, and poured it over my baby brother's head. You could hear the excess water run back into the font.

He said, "In the name of the Father, the Son, and the Holy Ghost, I, therefore, baptize you."

The baby did not even cry. The minister carefully returned the baby back to my mother. He finished reading his book and it was over.

Baptism

Even further, back in my memories, I remember having a baby doll with a christening dress. To this day, I have that doll on the top of my dresser in our bedroom.

Why, you may ask?

Why, you say? Fond memories and strong family traditions.

Why did my parents do all the preparations it took to set up a christening? The reason is that they wanted their baby to be safe. Heaven forbid if something happened to their baby before reaching the age of twelve, they would know the child would go to heaven.

I remember age twelve very well. I went to confirmation classes once a week for three months. I really only remember the last few classes when we practiced for the big day. The big day was Palm Sunday or Easter Sunday. The Bishop of the diocese was to be there. If I thought our minister's robes were special, the Bishop's robes were even better. He even wore a special triangle hat on his head. Throughout the service, he would take it off and then put it back on.

I wore a white dress. It did not matter if it was handed down from my sisters. It was beautiful. I had brand new white shoes and white socks. I do not remember having anything on my head, but I must have, because ladies were not allowed inside the sanctuary without something covering their head. However, I do remember that Sunday morning when all the girls sat together on the first three pews of the church. When we were given the signal, two girls at a time went to the front to meet the Bishop. He was sitting on a very tall back, red velvet chair. He had a staff in one hand. One girl knelt on one side and I knelt on the other. I had the side where he was holding the staff. He placed his free hand on the other girl's head. For an instant, I thought he might hit me with his staff. However, I did not have to worry; he lifted his free hand and touched my head. We were then motioned to stand up and return to our pew.

*****

If you were stranded on a Tropical Island and all you had was a Bible. . .

No, let us change that; you have heard that before.

What if you lived so far north, say outside Churchill, Manitoba, Canada, and you chose to live there in the wilderness? You have prepared your cabin for the upcoming winter.

Your wood is cut and neatly piled high around the outside and inside of your cabin. It is piled up under the few windows you have to look outside at the rest of the wilderness around you.

The harvest from your vegetable garden, which was good that year, is stored in your root cellar, right below the floor, you are now standing on.

Baptism

The moose and deer meat, results of a great hunting season, are dressed and are hanging in the tool shed. The meat is already frozen because the frost came early this year. You even made floor rugs of the moose and deer hides.

You placed steel bars on the windows and larger spikes on the doors of the cabin and tool shed. The doors resembled porcupines, but no polar bears were going to get through.

You are ready for the first snow blizzard. In fact, the snow is flying and the wind is howling, as you sit in the homemade rocker beside your wood stove. You and man's best friend 'Wolf' is looking forward to the long winter ahead. You have but one thing to read, the old family Bible.

The question is what will you learn about you and God? No one is there to tell you his or her beliefs and their traditions. You would actually find out what God wants you to do. He wants a personal relationship with you. That is what He wants from all of us.

It will surprise you what you will not find in the Bible.

- Jesus was the archangel Michael.
- Jesus was the prophet Mohammed.
- Jesus told Mr. Smith there was a lost book.
- The pope is your only intercessor to God.
- If you give money, you can buy your way into heaven

- If you go to confession on Friday, you can dowhat you want on the weekend.
- All good people are going to Heaven.
- Jesus was born on Christmas Day.
- It does not matter what God we believe in because we are all going to the same place - heaven - just a different road to get there.
- Money is the root of all evil.
- God is out to get you, He is just waiting for you to make a mistake and then it is all over.
- And yes, even Christening and Confirmation.

All this stuff we have heard throughout our lifetime. It is not in the Bible. You have to be told about it by some man. It is not from God.

So what about Christening? How can that be so bad? It is such a sweet thing. A baby dressed in white. Parents doing what they think is right to protect their baby and keep him safe.

Let us go back to where you are sitting in your homemade rocking chair and Wolf is lying at your feet, he does not hear any polar bears close by. The wind is still howling and the snow is still flying. However, you are warm and protected by your little cabin and the fire is crackling in the woodstove. You are reading the family Bible.

You are reading Psalm 139:13-16. You see what God thinks of young children. God knew David even before he was born.

"For you created my inmost being; you knit me together in my mother's womb. I praise you because I am fearfully made. Your works are wonderful, I know that full well. My frame was not hidden from you when I was made in the secret place. When I was woven together in the depths of the earth, your eyes saw my unformed body."

Then you turn to Matthew 18:1-6.

"At that time, the disciples came to Jesus and asked, "Who is the greatest in the kingdom of heaven?" He called a little child and had him stand among them. And he said: "I tell you the truth, unless you change and become like little children, you will never enter the kingdom of heaven. Therefore, whoever humbles himself like this child is the greatest in the kingdom of heaven. And whoever welcomes a little child like this in my name welcomes me. But if anyone causes one of these little ones who believe in me to sin, it would be better for him to have a large millstone hung around his neck and to be drowned in the depths of the sea."

It seems to me that it is very clear that Jesus loves children. He took time out of His very busy schedule to be with them. He even said, "Let the little children come unto me. . ." Children from birth to the age of accountability are protected by Jesus Himself. Safe in the arms of Jesus and we should have no fear, for they have an open door policy to Heaven.

What is baptism? Baptism is an act that a sinner does to break the separation from God that sin has made between the person and God. All people are sinners. Yes, you and I. The only one who is without sin is Jesus who lived on this earth a perfect life. If sin separates us from God, then how do we get back to Him? Jesus died on the cross, and on the third day, was raised from the dead. Doing this He took away all my sins.

You continue reading from Romans 6:3:

". . . don't you know that all of us who were baptized into Christ Jesus were baptized into his death? We were therefore buried with him through baptism into death in order that, just as Christ was raised from the dead through the glory of the Father, we too may live a new life."

Next, I want you to read Acts 2:38, where Peter replied:

> "Repent and be baptized, every one of you, in the name of Jesus Christ for the forgiveness of your sins, And you will receive the gift of the Holy Spirit."

Then turn to Acts 8:26-40. Read the whole story of Philip and the Ethiopian. Here you will see how baptism took place. Take note that Philip and this important official of Ethiopia left the chariot when he said, "Look, here is water. Why shouldn't I be baptized?" Then both Philip and the eunuch went down into the water and Philip baptized him. When they came up out of the water, the Spirit of the Lord suddenly took Philip away, and the eunuch did not see him again, but went on his way rejoicing."

Jesus told His disciples the great commission in Mark 16:14-18.

> "Go into the entire world and preach the good news to all creation. Whoever believes and is baptized will be saved, but whoever does not believe will be condemned."

There are many other places you can read about baptism in the Bible. The ones we have just studied show many things.

1. They were all adults that were baptized.
2. They had to be taught. Hear the good news of Christ.
3. They had to believe what Christ did for them.
4. They had to repent. We all have sinned and repenting of our sins is necessary.
5. They all had to go down into the water.
6. They all came back up out of the water.
7. They all went away rejoicing because their sins were taken away.

All the above a baby cannot do, nor does he need to.

Where did christening come from? Where, when and who started it? And why?

We believe it started around the year A.D. 250. The leaders at that time believed that humans were born with a fallen nature and tainted by original sin. Adam and Eve's sin was passed down to all mankind. Therefore, they reasoned that babies are born in sin. However, the only thing original sin is, is that it originates in the hearts of men. Baptism is for those who have repented of their sins Babies are not sinners. The doctrine of inherited sin or total depravity is not supported by scripture. Ezekiel 18:20 illustrates that the punishment of sin is not transferred to others.

> The soul who sins is the one who will die. The son will not share the guilt of the father, nor will the father share the guilt of the son. The

righteousness of the righteous man will be credited to him, and the wickedness of the wicked will be charged against him.

Boy, am I thankful. I have problems enough taking care of my own sins. To have to worry about taking care of my parents', grandparents' and great-grandparents' sins would be overwhelming.

My question is, "By whose authority do we baptize infants? Certainly not by God's authority."

Those who advocate infant baptism cite the book of Acts, where whole households were baptized. They assume the word "household" includes babies. This is just that: an assumption. The word household could include teenagers or even grown children. Some of these people, Lydia, Cornelius, and Crispus, were people of position and wealth. Household to them would include servants and their families.

Those in the household, whoever it is, heard words "by which you will be saved, you and your household."[26] Babies are not able to understand and accept the gospel of Christ. "Crispus the synagogue ruler, and his entire household believed in the Lord."[27] A baby cannot believe the preached word. The household of Stephanas "devoted themselves to the service of the saints.[28] Infants are incapable of such a task.

The Bible never shows baptism being used as a "pledge" or a "promise" to adults. It is not used as a sign to bring a child up in a godly way. In the New Testament, baptism is an immersion into Jesus Christ. It removes sin[29] and is for salvation. [30]

Baptism is the beginning point of becoming a Christian, a new birth, a new creature in Christ. You are free from sin. As you live your Christian life, the blood of Christ continues to cleanse you.

The celebrating begins as soon as you come up out of the water. The angels in heaven are singing in celebration. Christian friends are clapping their hands and stand in a circle singing, "Bind Us Together Lord. . ."

Your journey has not ended when you are baptized; it is the beginning. The service to Jesus has just begun.

Dear God,

Thank you for the Bible. I pray that men and women, girls and boys everywhere will take the time to read and study it.

The Word of God. Just to say it is amazing.

Reading the Bible is the closest time we will get to You on earth. It is my communication link between You and me. Your plan for Your children is spelled out within the pages of this book.

Let man not pollute it! Let man not say, "This part is not important or that this part is more important. Or, God didn't mean what He said, for I know what God really meant; therefore, I am going to change it."

God, you do not need any help. Since You created everything, surely You can tell us what You mean. We just need to listen.

Your Word was given in love. God, You gave us a choice to live through Your guidelines, or "Go your own way".

I have tried "Going your own way" route. It took me a long time to figure out why I was so unhappy.

Guide me through the journey of Life.

Thank you, God.

In Jesus Name,

Catherine Wilcoxson

DeQuincy Railroad Museum
DeQuincy, Louisiana

CHAPTER 9 CARS, PLANES, TRAINS AND FEET

Many times, I have heard my husband Paul say, "I do not like to drive. If anyone else is willing to drive, I would be just fine sitting in the back seat."

Paul was not blessed with a wife who feels comfortable driving in heavy traffic in large cities. Not that I could not if I really had to. One of those occasions happened just recently. Christopher and Kayla were expecting their first baby. Christopher, being a preacher's kid, accepted the fact that his parents would not be around to visit them on Sundays. The whole family accepted this.

I received a special invitation to a baby shower in Cincinnati, Ohio. It was to be on a Sunday afternoon. The shower was for Lily, and since Lily was to be my first granddaughter, nothing was going to keep me away. Paul was unavailable to take me since it was on a Sunday. He had three services and a special dinner to attend.

I prayed and prayed, "God, I can do this, I can drive myself there. I can do this, can't I, God?" The only thing in my way was the cities of Indianapolis and Cincinnati. It was only a three-hour drive. The time was not a problem; the traffic was.

I did it! What a feeling of accomplishment. I was like a little girl who just learned to tie her shoes or ride a two-wheeler bike. I did it! I stepped out of my comfort zone, and with God's help, (I prayed a lot) it was done. I used a G.P.S., and my steering wheel was covered with yellow stick-on notes telling me what turns to take. Christopher met me in his driveway. He knew this was not an easy thing for me to do. We celebrated together, and I allowed him to do the driving the rest of the weekend while I was there in Cincinnati.

I enjoyed Lily's baby shower; I delivered a letter to Kayla from Lily's three cousins Logan, Ethan, and Connor, welcoming her into our family. I enjoyed watching my daughter-in-law with child, carrying this precious gift from God. She would soon be a mother, and a good mother she would be.

When God opens doors, even if it is out of our comfort zones He wants us to trust Him and walk through.

Cars, Planes. Trains, and Feet

*****

For Paul to say he does not like driving, we seem to take many trips by car. The first trip I can remember was in December 1974. I had just received my driver's license in October of the same year. I had only known Paul for a short time and here he was allowing me to drive his car, while he was sitting beside me in the front seat playing the guitar. We were headed to Sheet Harbour to visit my parents for Christmas. That was the time we fell in love and we have had 36 years of car trips since. Many trips from Ontario to Nova Scotia. Trips to Tennessee, Alabama, Louisiana, California and driving through the States in between. We have lived in six states and two provinces of Canada. Just keeping up with visiting family has kept us on the road.

Sometimes living so far away, the only option to visit loved ones is to fly. Some people love to fly on an airplane. I have the opinion that I can tolerate it. It is something that must be done, so I do it. I figure I can do anything for one day.

My problem is more claustrophobic, rather the fear of crashing. My attitude is that the pilot wants to go home for dinner as much as I want to get to my designation. However, to slide into one of those small seats and stay there for hours takes a lot of talking to myself, and, of course, talking to God.

Everyone has a story to tell of experiencing turbulence. On one of our plane trips, the plane dropped several hundred feet. Dishes, bags and everything not tied down went flying. A gentleman who had the misfortune of walking up the aisle at this time, fell into the empty seat beside me and quickly fastened his safety belt. At the same moment, I looked towards Paul, who was holding onto the windowsill of the plane with dear life. For some reason I thought it was funny and told him, "Sorry, honey, that window sill is coming with you." He was not amused.

The era after 9-11-01 can make going through security a nightmare. The metal detector machine can be very intimidating. When the bells and sirens go off, you look around to see what you have done wrong. For some reason, Paul makes the metal detector go off more than not. Of course, this happens when one is in a very big hurry and you are running late for a flight.

This is what happened at the New York airport. The bells and sirens were going off. Two inspector officers sat Paul in a chair and with a wand detector started going over him.

"Hands up, hands down, stand up, sit down, unbutton your jeans, pull your zipper down."

By this time Paul was very concerned, he thought for sure the next command would be, "Drop your pants." Paul did not know why the alarm kept going off, but it was obvious these two men were going to find the answer. Finally, after about ten minutes, they gave up and let Paul continue on his journey. As he walked away, they could be heard saying, "Have a nice Flight."

Cars, Planes. Trains, and Feet

Paul did not think they were the nicest two men he had ever met. It took him a long time to get over that experience. It was enough to make him enjoy driving a car.

*****

What about trains?

People do not travel by train very often. Today trains are used more for carrying freight than anything else. Nevertheless, there are routes people can use for transportation.

When Paul and I lived in San Marcos, California, we would take the double-decker train to San Diego. We made two trips: one for me to take the test to become a United States citizen and the other to be sworn in as a citizen. It was a beautiful ride along the Pacific Coast. It was not unusual to see surfers riding the waves as you traveled along.

Becoming a citizen of the United States of America was a privilege and honor and a very exciting time. It took several years of filling out papers, paying fees, being interviewed and having fingerprints taken. Finally, I had one more thing to do -- take a test. I studied for months to take the oral exam. It was hard for me to go into a room with a complete stranger, who was going to fire questions at me, and I would have to answer them correctly. However, I knew God would be sitting right beside me. In addition, I believe I knew more about the United

States government and how it worked than the average citizen walking down the street.

Now I belong to two countries. I did not have to give up my Canadian citizenship.

Trains were a larger part of our lives living in De Quincy, Louisiana. We did not ride the trains; we just had to wait for them to pass by. DeQuincy, being an historical railroad town, had three main railroad lines coming into the town in different directions. You got used to the sound of the train horns that blew day and night.

The DeQuincy Railroad Station was a quaint one indeed. It was built in 1923. The trains no longer stop in DeQuincy, but that did not stop the people who live there from figuring out a new use for their railroad station. They started a DeQuincy Railroad Days Festival. On the second weekend of April every year, people come from all around to attend the special festival. Thursday, Friday, and Saturday a carnival would set up their rides; booths were set up to sell great food and crafts. The Pentecostal Church booth sold hamburgers and they always had the longest line. They were the best hamburgers in all of southern Louisiana.

When we first moved to DeQuincy, Paul started a publication called "On the Right Track." It was inserted into the "The DeQuincy News" with the grocery ads and other advertisements six times a year. During the Rail Road Festival, we made a float for the parade and an "On the Right Track" booth.

I believe the DeQuincy Railroad Festival was the only train festival that had real trains passing through. I was always afraid someone was going to be run over by a train, but that did not seem to concern those living in DeQuincy. The trains always slowed down and blew their horn in a greeting, and the engineer always waved as they passed by. Conductors were even seen walking in front of their trains waving a red flag. Children just seemed to know to stay out of the way.

In the heyday of the railroad town of DeQuincy, there was a round table. It was a large rail yard where all the engines were brought for repair. That too faded away. The Kansas City Railroad deeded the property over to the city. Today, this same property has been changed into a baseball park complex. It includes a playground and a walking trail.

Many people thought DeQuincy would turn into a ghost town when the railroad left. However, it makes me think of the people in America that say America is no longer a Christian nation. They believe that Christianity is dying out. However, I have faith and believe that people will not forget the Savior of this world. Satan will not win.

Hard work is what is needed. Just like the people of DeQuincy, they would not let their town die. Sure, they had hard times. It took hard work to come back from the railroad leaving. It will take hard work for Christians to shine their lights. We have to be watchful for those who would try to snuff out our lights.

DeQuincy was brought to its knees again. 'Rita' made a visit. That is another story to tell. You can read of that in my chapter on 'Weather'.

*****

How would Jesus have fit into today's world?

What kind of a car would He have driven?

Just imagine how many places He could have visited. How many more people could have been healed?

Would He have been annoyed to go through the metal detector at the airport? Would He have cleared security with a shout or a crack of his whip?

Can you picture Him sitting on a train and teaching the passengers around Him?

All Jesus had was feet. His feet and donkey feet. He went out in the surrounding area teaching and preaching to the lost.

How far have you ever walked?

Three miles seems like a long way. Would we leave the house and walk three miles to the mall? Unlikely. More likely, we would be looking for the car keys and then jump into the car.

We do not use our feet for transportation.

That is all Jesus had! Feet, and on occasion, maybe, a donkey. However, He mostly walked.

Cars, Planes. Trains, and Feet

Jesus made a trip. The story is told with many details. It begins when Jesus decided to leave Judea and go to Samaria. He knew the Pharisees had heard and were talking about that He was baptizing a great number of people. This was the beginning of the Pharisees being unhappy about this man Jesus, for they did not like Jesus at all.

I can see the Pharisees' meetings now. Questions being asked all around the room.

"Who is this man called Jesus?"

"Where is He from?"

"Jesus of Nazareth."

"Nazareth? Is there any good that comes from Nazareth?"

"Jesus is the son of a carpenter."

"John the baptizer called him the Lamb of God. You know the one who preached to the crowds in the wilderness."

"He is the one who ate honey and locusts and looked like a wild man, wearing skins of animals."

"Not only that, there are stories going around Jesus turned water to wine at some wedding in Cana."

"We all heard what happened in the Temple. He disrupted the moneychangers in the women's court. He drove them all out, yelling something about this was his father's house. We lost a lot of money that day."

"Jesus has more followers every day."

"Well, we need to make a stop to all of this. See to it that He is watched."

*****

Politics. We all think of many different things when the word politics is mentioned. However, one thing politicians are famous for is never getting their facts completely straight. It was no different in Jesus' time. One fact the Pharisees did not get right was Jesus did not do the baptizing; His disciples did. Jesus did not want anyone to think that if He did the baptizing, it was more important than anyone else who baptized. Therefore, Jesus did not baptize people.

Jesus knew the Pharisees were talking about Him. His disciples may not have known, but Jesus knew. No one had to tell Him. He also knew it would get worse, and the malice of the Pharisees would grow rapidly as to endanger his life.

Jesus was not finished with His ministry. He could probably do as much good in Galilee, as in Judea. He planned His trip to Galilee.

Jesus pulled out his maps and his G.P.S. He knew it was 34 miles to Galilee from Jerusalem, but His G.P.S. detoured Him to a different route. 'Jews do not go through Samaria' was

Cars, Planes. Trains, and Feet

written on his map. Instead, His G.P.S. directed Him to a circuitous route on the east side of the Jordan.

Jesus and His disciples started out early in the day. After a period of time, a familiar sound was heard.

"Recalculating! Recalculating!"

Jesus was not taking the route on the east side of the Jordan. He was going straight through Samaria.

Jesus and His disciples arrived in the city of Sychar. It was one of the oldest cities of Palestine. Jesus knew the history of this place. It was here that Joshua assembled the people before his death, and here they renewed their covenant with the Lord. In addition, it was here the bones of Joseph were buried when they were brought up from Egypt. This was near to the homestead of Jacob.

G.P.S. sounded again. "Arriving at via point."

The rest stops of rest stops. Jesus was stopping at Jacob's well.

Have you ever stopped at a rest stop, and getting out of the car, your legs are so stiff you walk a little funny, as you make your way toward the public buildings? You are tired and in need of refreshing.

Jesus stopped at the well. He was wearied.

That is an understatement. He had just walked more than 30 miles. Some of my research indicated He did so without taking a break.

He reached the well at the sixth hour, which was noonday. This was the common time of the Jewish meal. Jesus instructed His disciples to continue into the city to buy food. He sat down at the well, for its location was on the outside of the city.

Jesus watched as a Samaritan woman came towards the well to draw water.

"Give me a drink, for the heat of a noonday sun has parched my lips," He said.

Have you ever been thirsty? I do not think very many people reading this book have been truly thirsty. The first sign of thirst we go to our fridge for cold water. Or we drink from the bottled water we carry everywhere we go. I do not believe we have ever had parched lips from thirst.

Jesus did!

He had a problem. Even though He was sitting by a well, and knew there was water, He had no way to get to it. For some reason, Jesus did not have a jar made of skin with him. All travelers at this time carried such a jar. It was more important than maps and G.P.S. devices today. Your jar made of animal skin would allow you to draw water from the wells that were sparsely scattered throughout the desert of the region.

The woman was startled.

In the first place, she felt nervous seeing a Jewish man sitting by the well. She probably thought to herself whether she should even go about her task drawing water, or maybe she should return later. She decided to go quietly about her task.

She probably jumped two feet when the request came.

"Give me a drink."

She knew very well that Jewish men did not speak to women in public. Furthermore, she knew they would never speak to a Samaritan. She knew her people were referred to as 'dogs' by the Jews. She was surprised to see a Jewish man sitting at the well in the first place. Jews never entered her land.

Her response was a natural one. "How is it that you being a Jew, ask me for a drink since I am a Samaritan woman?"

Jesus' answer was very perplexing indeed. "If you knew the gift of God, and who it is that asks you for a drink, you would have asked Him and He would have given you living water."

"How are you going to get this living water you speak of? You have nothing to draw with."

"Everyone who drinks of this water will thirst again; but whoever drinks of the water that I will give him will become in him a well of water springing up to eternal life."

"Now that is what I need. I need some of this water you speak of, so I will no longer thirst."

She was tired of coming to the well at the hottest time of the day, each and every day. She did not understand such water, but she wanted some.

Jesus changed the subject. "Go call your husband."

"I have no husband."

Jesus said, "You have correctly said 'I have no husband', for you have had five husbands, and the one whom you now have is not your husband."

"Sir, I perceive that you are a prophet."

Jesus was showing her He was acquainted with her life and with her sins. Even though He was a stranger and knew her life, this convinced her that He was qualified to teach the way to heaven.

Seeing herself revealed, does she admit to her wrongdoing?

No. She changes the subject.

This woman has probably heard men discuss the big question. There was a dispute between the Samaritan people and the Jews. She, being around men, quickly thinks of how this great prophet, she has just met can be of service to her. Nor did she want to discuss her private life with this stranger, so she quickly changes the subject and asks the question.

"You know our fathers worship on this mountain, and you people say that in Jerusalem is the place where men ought to worship, what is your opinion?"

Jesus sides with the Jews and says, "You do not know what you worship. You have no authority and you are in the dark. For salvation is of the Jews."

"But the hour is coming when the old way will pass away and the new way begin for all who truly and sincerely worship God. They will do it from the heart, and not merely in words alone."

She then tells Him, "I know that the Messiah is coming."

She has heard it all her life, for the Samaritans acknowledged the five books of Moses, which teaches the coming of the Messiah.

Jesus words follow, "I who speak to you am He."

Doesn't this amaze you?!

This is the first time Jesus openly professed it. "I am the Messiah."

When does He choose to reveal this news?

The time is when He has just finished running a marathon. His lips are parched from thirst; His feet must be killing Him. He is sitting beside a well, where He cannot get to the water. He is talking to a Samaritan woman, the lowest class of people on the earth. Not even a good Samaritan woman at that. She comes to the well at the hottest time of the day for a reason. No other woman would allow her in their midst. She has had five husbands, and the one she now has is not even a husband.

Jesus chose her to tell of the greatest news ever told on this earth.

'Jesus was the Messiah!'

The greatest news of the world was not told to kings or the rich. It was not even told to His best friends. It was told to this woman at the well.

Then the moment is broken.

Gone.

What was she thinking?

We do not know yet. They were disturbed.

Just when the conversation was getting good, she heard words she would never forget. Just when she needed to know more, the spell was broken. They were interrupted.

The disciples came back. They had their grocery bags with them. Maybe some bread and fish. They were tired. They were on this same marathon with Jesus. Jesus got to rest. They had to go grocery shopping.

They were not too tired to notice that Jesus was talking, actually talking to a woman. They rubbed their eyes twice. Sure enough, Jesus was talking to a woman, not just a woman, a Samaritan woman. And they were amazed.

They did not say a word. If it had been anyone besides Jesus, they would have taken the man to task. Nevertheless, Jesus did things before that made them speechless. They saw him change water into wine. They saw him heal Peter's mother-in-law.

Cars, Planes, Trains, and Feet

And now this.

They did not ask why?

The Samaritan woman was jolted into action. It is the same as someone yelling, 'FIRE'. You not only listen you take action. You leave everything behind and make sure others hear the word 'FIRE'.

The Samaritan woman heard the word 'Messiah' run repeatedly in her mind. In addition, she believed Jesus was He. She left all the everyday tasks of surviving behind. She left her water pot and went into the city.

The Samaritan woman had one thing on her mind. She was focused. She had to tell everyone, even the ones that did not like her. I don't know how she did it, but she was convincing enough that she brought several back with her to the well to meet Jesus. Not just anyone, but the important people of the town. These people invited Jesus to stay and teach.[31]

I marvel at this woman at the well. She is a tough lady; she knew exactly who to take her good news to, and she did it. She didn't seem to care what people thought of her.

Whatever mode of travel you take whether by car, plane, train or feet; use them for the glory of God while telling the story of Jesus.

Our Wedding

March 14, 1975

DeQuincy, Louisiana

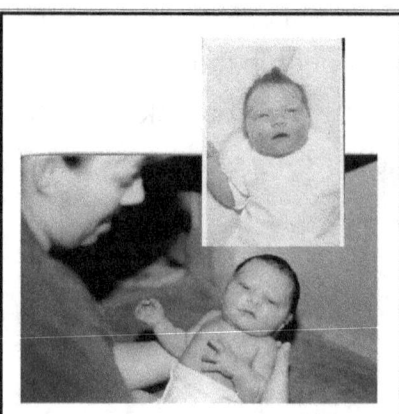

Didn't I Tell You These Two Babies Looked Just Alike?

Cars, Planes. Trains, and Feet

Open Doors and Open Windows: Journey with God

Cars, Planes, Trains, and Feet

First Home We Owned
Mill Village, N. S., Canada

DeQuincy Church of Christ Building,
DeQuincy, Louisiana

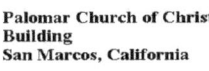

Jena Church of Christ Building
Jena, Louisiana

Palomar Church of Christ Building
San Marcos, California

Cars, Planes. Trains, and Feet

Dear God,

Thank You for our car. Let us use it for Your glory.

You have guided us to many places where we never could go without our car. We have seen the "promised land" of sorts. We have seen such a small part of Your beautiful world. You made this beauty just for my eyes to see. I stand in awe of You. The power of the oceans, the height of the mountains, the calmness of the great prairie. I look upon the beauty and I can say to the whole world, "MY GOD DID THIS." Just look what He did. I could go on and on, God, but changing the subject.

Politics. Lord, when You were here on earth, You saw how man tried to run the place. Politics can get pretty bad. Jesus, it has not changed much. I know that is why You asked us to pray for our leaders. They need all the help they can get. I pray for the leaders of our land.

Thank You, Jesus, for leaving us the details and stories of the many journeys You had while You were here. Thank You for telling us about the "Woman at the Well". We can learn so much about that time.

Thank you, Jesus, for being man. You understand our struggles because You experienced them Thank You for taking away my sin and bringing me back to our Father.

I pray in Your Name, Jesus.
Catherine Wilcoxson

St. Thomas, Ontario, Canada

CHAPTER 10 WEATHER

Do you ever stop and think about weather?

We do it every day. Sometimes more than once a day. Before we get dressed in the morning, we check the weather forecast. Is it going to be cold, or warm? Is it going to rain, or even snow? I love weather. Everyone needs to stop for a moment and see how special weather is. Good weather and bad weather and weather in between. Waking up to a sunny day – why even the birds are happily singing. We know it is going to be a good day. Maybe a good day for working outside planting flowers or tomatoes or cutting the grass.

Can you name your local weatherman?

Sure, you can. You want him to tell you it is going to be sunny on the weekend, so you and your family can get outside and enjoy God's great creation. If it is going to rain, and it will, we want it to do so in the middle of the week. That is if you are not on vacation. Being from Nova Scotia, weather can be a changeable thing. Summers are short; you make sure you enjoy the warm sunshine while you have it. Everyone sits on his porch in the long evenings.

Summer for me was spent in the cabin in Sheet Harbour, swimming every day and just playing in the outdoors. No TV. Back then, in the summer it was all re-runs anyway. After breakfast, mother's instructions were to be home at supper. That gave me six hours of freedom.

I would begin with a visit to my grandmother, Catherine. She lived in a small cottage about five minutes away. If it were not raining, she would be expecting me. She would sit in her rocking chair and I in another. I can picture her now. She had grey-white hair with a round face, kind eyes and a loving smile. She was a little on the heavy side, but I do not remember her being fat. She looked like a perfect grandmother to me. I wish I could remember all the stories she told. Only a few remain with me. Like the story of the Indian attack in Watt Section where she raised a dozen children. Or my favorite story of the ghost schooner that sailed by the lighthouse on a foggy night.

Grammy would tell me about my father growing up. She showed me a picture of my grandfather who was gone

Weather

before I was born. I remember that the picture looked just like my father.

I did not know how much time had passed, but I would then skip across the gravel driveway to visit Aunt Pearl and Uncle Gerald. It was lunchtime and they would be in their country kitchen. They always made me feel welcome, and I always left with a snack in my pocket.

My best friends would then appear, Elizabeth and Cathy. We would dress up in ladies' dresses with hats and high heels. Of course, Aunt Pearl provided me with a shiny maroon coloured dress, a hat, and a pair of heels to match. We would walk down the main road and tourists in RV's would stop and take our picture.

Other days we would run across a hayfield to climb on the gate. We also passed many hours playing in my playhouse. Across from the cabin was an acre of alder trees. The alder tree was called a nuisance tree. They were the first thing to grow in a neglected field. Alders had a small trunk and grew around 10-12 feet tall. My father took his axe and cut an entranceway into the forest of alders. Then he cleared three small rooms. A perfect playhouse with a shady roof protected from the afternoon sun. My father made furniture for us from the woodpile. Until needed, the logs made tables, chairs and baby doll beds. Of course, on a rainy day, everything was wet. However, while the summer sun shone, we spent many hours in my playhouse taking care of our baby dolls.

The most important thing to do was watch for high tide. The ocean's tide would change every day and we always swam at high tide. We would swim for hours in the summer sunshine.

*****

What about rain and storms? Rain makes you appreciate the sun. In Texas, people take the sun for granted. Most of the summer you wake up to sun and blue skies as far as you could see. Oh, yes, and heat. Every day is the same.

Rain windstorms can get ugly. They call them hurricanes. The first hurricane I can remember was when Paul and I were first married and we lived in Shubenacadie, Nova Scotia. The weatherman did not even report a hurricane coming. It was upon us and everyone took notice. The windows of our apartment were rattling, but we got into our car for the planned trip to Halifax. On the highway, we saw trees falling on the side of the road. The wind blew so hard Paul was driving the car at 90 miles an hour against the wind to keep it from going off the road. We were not going 90 miles an hour, but the speedometer was recording it.

Weather

Nova Scotia's hurricanes are always the tail end of the storm. They are born in the Gulf of Mexico. We lived on the Gulf of Mexico in Louisiana for several years. For seven years the Gulf was quiet, no big hurricanes had hit for about 20 years. That changed in between moves from California, Jena, Louisiana and Covington, Indiana. Remember, preachers come and preachers go.

We moved into Jena, Louisiana the same day that Hurricane Katrina hit. Katrina's direct hit was further east at New Orleans and Baton Rouge area. We were in the migration of people running from the coast. The next several weeks we were very busy helping those who lost everything in that terrible storm. People from the northern states and all over Canada sent Paul and me money. They knew we would insure that the money given went to good use.

It seems to me humans, or people, in general, do not do well in extreme environments. People, including our leaders, seem to lose their common sense. When life is easy, which it is for you and me, we live in a false sense of security. However, if everything around you turned upside down, would you be ready for it? You will never know that until it happens. I do think it is something to stop and think about. What would you do?

There are many nightmare stories told about Hurricane Katrina. Let me tell you two of ours.

Remember how thousands of people were stuck in the football stadium in New Orleans without food, electricity, which meant no air conditioning in 100 degrees temperatures? I remember well the call went throughout the state. The government was closing all schools and sending all school buses in the direction of New Orleans. We are talking hundreds, if not thousands, of buses. Jena's buses went. The people of Jena prepared for the arrival of bus loads of people. So did every other town that sent buses. Two days later, the buses came back empty. Turned out the police would not let the bus drivers near the stadium. The red tape was so thick that they would not allow people on the buses without filling out papers. Papers they did not even have. The same people who were dying inside the stadium.

How could this happen in the USA?

They lost their common sense. Instead of filling up buses and taking them back to their home, where then they could fill out papers, people suffered and people died.

A group of members of the Jena Church of Christ filled up two cars with supplies. We were told to go to a camp where refugees from the storm were staying. The Red Cross was set up there. The army was also there. When we arrived at the gate, we were told to put our items in the gym. When we got there, the gym was stacked from the floor to the ceiling with donated stuff. Half the gym was full.

I asked one question, "How long has this stuff been here?"

They answered, "Five days."

Paul and I looked at each other and told our group to get back in the cars. We certainly were not going to leave our carefully gathered supplies there. We knew where people needed the help, and we took it to them personally.

Are you ready for something like Katrina to happen? Are you ready to take care of yourself for weeks at a time, depending on no one but you and God?

Katrina was the worst hurricanes we have ever seen, but Rita and Gustav came after. We watched Hurricane Rita pass by in the darkness of our home. Jennifer and our two grandsons ran from the coast. In darkness and 100 degrees temperatures, we sat playing cards by candlelight. With our back door open to get air as the rain pelted down, we listened to the wind as the trees swayed back and forth.

Hurricane Rita did a lot of damage to DeQuincy, Louisiana. Every roof was damaged. Blue tarps were placed on roofs to keep the rain out. The colour blue on roofs lasted many months. There were not enough workers to replace tiles on roofs, and stores were closed for a long time.

Because of Katrina, Rita, and the damage they caused, when Hurricane Gustav came along, everyone was told to leave. By this time, Paul and I lived in Covington, Indiana. Jennifer, Michael and our grandsons still lived in DeQuincy. We had another great concern; Jennifer was due to have our third grandson the same time Gustav was to hit the Gulf Coast.

With the blessings of Orchard Hills Church of Christ, we quickly packed our car and made a trip to Louisiana to rescue our kids from the hurricane. It takes two days traveling to get from Covington to DeQuincy, Louisiana. It is a good thing you get a week's warning of a hurricane coming.

It is amazing, a hurricane is the only weather phenomenon that you can prepare for. You have warnings, and you can get ready. When you are a sailor and a storm is approaching, you batten down the hatches. That means you tie down anything that may come loose. The same is true in a hurricane, especially if you live on the Gulf Coast. You pick up or tie down anything that could blow away. Boarding up windows is a good idea. Years ago, people would place tape on windows in the design of a cross or an x to keep the windows from breaking. It was determined that it really did not help much. All it did was cause a sticky mess that was very hard to remove.

Weather

Paul and I arrived in Louisiana two days later. We were just in time to head to the hospital. Jennifer was induced that morning, and we were just in time for Connor Matthew Boyle to be born. Jennifer was not the only mother who had a baby that night; 27 other babies had help coming into this world before Gustav the hurricane arrived.

The next morning we were on our way to the hospital to visit the new mommy and Connor. All I can remember is that it was very hot. Close to 100 degrees and the humidity close to 100%. In the parking lot of the hospital, it was even hotter, and the sun shining on new concrete caused a bright glare. It was very hard to see. I was looking for our son-in-law's car, when without realizing it, my foot stepped off the sidewalk and I went down. Anytime you fall, everything seems to move in slow motion. The side of my face and head bounced off the new cement. As Paul helped pick me up, we could see that my glasses caused a gash in my temple close to my eye.

Instead of visiting my new grandson, I was now in the ER. No one was happy, especially me. I was so mad at myself; all I wanted to do was go upstairs and hold baby Connor. The hospital staff was not too happy either. They were evacuating all patients from the hospital; they did not need a new patient.

Repeatedly I said, "Put a band-aid on it and let me go upstairs."

After a couple of hours, they finally allowed me to go upstairs. This was Friday, and that afternoon, the official evacuation order was called. Everyone had to leave. Gustav was coming straight for us and would make landfall Monday morning.

We had another big problem. The hospital would not discharge Jennifer until Saturday. In the meantime, Paul, and I had our grandsons, Logan and Ethan, at Smokey Cove in a cabin. I was nursing a headache.

Sunday morning, I remember waking up talking to God.

"Lord, I can't go to worship You today. God, I have these two precious boys to take care of. I do not know what today will bring. Jesus, be with us. Show us the way and keep us safe. God, we will have Michael, Jennifer and baby Connor with us. We are going to need Your help. I feel the need of Your presence. Give me strength, God. In Jesus' name, I pray this prayer, Amen."

We met Michael, Jennifer and baby Connor twelve miles outside of DeQuincy going north along the Hurricane Evacuation Route. They were in a white van packed with things they did not want to leave behind, including a dog, a cat, and a brand new baby. It was a hot day in Louisiana and the traffic was heavy, all going north away from the

Weather

coast. People were pulling boats, trailers, and their cars full of personal possessions, all they could carry.

It was one large migration. We were all going in one direction. Not a car on the other side of the road. In fact, when we entered the small towns, the army was there, actually carrying rifles. Both sides of the road were turned to go in one direction. The soldiers wanted us to keep up and go one direction only; they did not want us to stop. You felt like you were part of a movie, but this was no movie; this was real life.

We were a two-car caravan. The boys were with Paul and me in our car. Jennifer, Michael and baby Connor with a dog and cat followed in a van. We talked to one another through cell phones. An hour into our slow journey, we were informed it was time to stop and feed Connor. Jennifer was nursing. Wal-Mart seemed to be the best place to stop. Nannie and Papa took the boys inside to visit the toy section. We even let them try riding the bikes up and down the aisle. An hour later, our caravan joined the migration north, following everyone else away from the coast.

The problem with running from a hurricane is that everyone else is running also. Our society is not made for everyone to use gas stations and hotels at the same time. It does not take long for gas stations to run out of gas. Those that still have gasoline jack up the prices; everyone is into making a lot of money.

Hotel rooms are impossible to find. We were already two hours from the coast, safe enough to ride out the storm, but there was not anywhere to stay. We had heard the closest hotel room was in St. Louis, a two-day drive. Knowing this problem, we had made plans to go to Memphis, an eight-hour drive from DeQuincy.

Paul and I had lived in Memphis. We had good friends there. Jean and the ladies of the White Station Church of Christ were waiting for us. They had prepared places for us and the pets to stay.

We stopped at the welcome center entering Mississippi. It was hot and very crowded. We tried to fix sandwiches in the parking lot for everyone. That was miserable, like working inside an oven. Jennifer was in tears; her feet and legs were swelling. We gave up, put everything and everybody back in the cars and headed back down the road. At least we had air conditioning in the car.

Just as we entered Vicksburg, Michael called; Jennifer was crying and could not go any further. I just said, "Okay," and seeing a sign in front of me that read McDonald's at the next exit, we took the exit and headed for McDonald's.

Weather

I ran to Jennifer; she was in bad shape. She could not stop crying, and her feet and ankles were swollen three times larger than they should be. This young mother, who had just given birth less than 48 hours before, should not be traveling in a van when it was 100 degrees. We still had five hours to go to reach Memphis, maybe longer with the traffic.

God has blessed me with a gift. Any time there is an emergency I get stronger, take over, and deal with the emergency. My emergency mode kicked in because I saw fear in my daughter's eyes. I remember my words to this day.

"Okay, Jennifer, everything is going to be fine. I have a plan. We were going to take over McDonald's."

I do not know what she thought; I did not give her a chance. I grabbed two pillows from the van and helped her into McDonald's. To Michael and Paul, I said, "Bring the baby and the boys."

Now I want you to see God's power. God opened doors ahead of me; He was leading and I was following Him.

The first miracle to happen was we found an empty table in a corner. The place was crowded.

I put Jennifer on the bench with pillows under her feet. Jennifer was still crying, saying, "I can't go any further." To say the least, people were staring at us.

Taking Paul aside, we agreed the first thing to do was to see if there was a hotel room. Of course, I was not very optimistic, but we had to start somewhere. It did not take long for the news to spread throughout McDonald's that a newborn baby and the mother were camping out there. The employees were as helpful as they could be. Their store was crowded, and now they had a mother and a newborn, plus the rest of the family.

There were no hotel rooms, but hurricane shelters were now suggested. Most hurricane shelters have to be the closest thing to hell this side of eternity. That would be our last resort. Yes, you would be safe from the storm, but you do not know whether your closest neighbours are good or bad. Many times, they do not have the same moral values you share, and some can be downright nasty. In addition, I asked myself, "Are we going to take a newborn baby and new mother to that environment?" Germs alone scared me half to death.

I prayed that very moment, "God help us! Show us the way."

Paul got off the phone with a list of several shelters in the area. He looked at me and said, "Catherine, why don't we call the Church of Christ?"

Of course, God, and He were already making plans.

Weather

Sure enough, there was a Church of Christ five minutes away and they were setting up a Hurricane Evacuation Shelter. Paul and I agreed that is where we were going. In the meantime, let us feed everyone and then we will find the shelter. The boys were thrilled to eat French fries and chicken nuggets.

God knew we needed help. Up walked an older couple who were eating their lunch at McDonald's. They were from the area. He approached us and asked about Jennifer and the baby. When they heard our story and where we were going, they said, "We know where that church is; we will take you and get you settled." Angels, God sent us angels. I thought I was going to end up in tears, but I took one look at Jennifer and thought, "One lady crying is enough."

We gently put Jennifer and baby Connor back in the van and followed our angels. When we arrived, I left Jennifer feeding the baby and went inside. It was just after lunch; there were not very many people around.

The Red Cross was setting up the shelter and just using the church building. The Red Cross lady did not show that she understood our situation. All she wanted us to do was fill out papers. I left Paul to answer questions.

I finally was able to talk to a member of the church. He was helping with setting up the shelter. When he heard our story and my concern about putting Jennifer and baby in a public place, he agreed with me. Also, when I told him Paul was a minister of a Church of Christ, everything changed. He said they had a queen size mattress in the storage room. He would put it on the floor in the Teen Bible classroom, which was on the other side of the church building, separate from the shelter. The rest of the family could use the front foyer of the church.

"Thank you, God, you answer prayers."

I went back to find Paul still answering questions and filling out paperwork. When I told him the good news, I went to get Jennifer and tell her the plan. I started bringing in things we would need.

The Red Cross lady stopped me at the door. "I'm sorry, but you will not be able to stay on the other side of the church building," she said. "You must stay in the public section of the shelter."

Of course, my first reaction was, "Why?"

"Because," she said, "This is a Red Cross Shelter; I am in charge, and I cannot allow you to stay away from the general public."

All I can remember is seeing red. I took three steps towards that lady and said, "Lady, if you do not get out of my way, I will knock you down."

I do not remember if I actually said the last five words, but the lady stepped aside. The member of that church led me through two hallways to the other side of the church building. A private room was set up for Jennifer and baby Connor. We put both of them to bed.

The rain started and the wind blew. Gustav arrived. We were safe. It was now Sunday evening; worship was about to begin and we lived in the foyer.

Remember my prayer that morning. "God, I can't worship you today, be with us during this day. We have to run from this storm. Take care of us; we have Jennifer and a new baby. Please stay with us." And He did.

Worship was taking place one hundred feet from Jennifer's bedroom. The teens came in and were amazed their classroom had been turned into a nursery.

Paul, the boys, and I sat in our pew singing songs of praise to God who showed us the way this day. He brought us to safety to brothers and sisters in the Lord. We took communion, the Lord's Supper. The ushers delivered the unleavened bread and red grape juice to Jennifer and Michael, who were taking care of brand new little Connor in the teen classroom. The Lord's Supper represents the body and blood of Jesus, which He shed on the cross of Calvary.

I have always believed in answer to prayer. However, this was the first time I saw answers to prayer before it was even spoken. God allowed doors and windows to open in front of us, when we were in great danger, and He showed us the way. God sent angels before us. That older couple called us that evening. They wanted to know if they could bring a recliner for Jennifer to sit in. We thanked them and told them Jennifer was settled into a real bed.

I only have one regret. In all the commotion of the day, I did not get their names. I did not get a chance to write and say thank you.

Gustav made his presence known all through the night. I was on baby duty. Jennifer needed to rest. I walked little baby Connor up and down the dark foyer until he was asleep. Connor and I then slept on the back pew of the auditorium listening to the wind blow and the rain beating on the roof. I tried to rest. I kept one hand on the baby, for I was so afraid he would roll off. Connor slept well; my fear of him falling off the pew did not materialize.

Poor Jake the dog and Sarah the cat did not have it as comfortable as we did. They were not allowed inside the shelter. Michael tied Jake under children's play equipment, and Sarah the cat was in her crate just outside the door.

Morning came, the rain still fell in sheets and the wind blew branches and the leaves from the trees. Thanks to God, we were all safe. I made my way into the newly renovated ladies' room. It was so pretty, nicer than any hotel bathroom would have ever been. I looked in the mirror, and a reflection of the biggest black eye I had ever seen came back to me. I looked closer; it was a double ringer. Black, blue, yellow, and even a little green. With everything going on, I had forgotten the discomfort of my head and eye.

My grandsons were impressed. "Does it hurt, Nannie?" they asked.

We kept a low profile being on the other side of the building of a storm shelter. The shelter was packed. However, no one knew we were there. We did go over to eat our meals. The first meal I went to, the Red Cross lady met me. She wanted to know what happened to my eye in the middle of the night. She was sure someone had hit me.

I was thankful the Red Cross was around. They checked baby Connor and Jennifer daily. They also helped treat my eye. It was comforting to know that, when we needed it, medical help was close by. The ladies that volunteered at the shelter also made their daily visits to the new mother and baby. Baby Connor was never left alone. There was always someone with him, when we would go to the other side of the church building. Even though the Red Cross had hired security, there were moments we felt insecure.

Connor had his first bath in the new renovated ladies' bathroom. We spent long hours waiting for Gustav to leave. The boys watched movies on Papa's laptop computer. I worked on a new quilt. Connor did what new babies do best. He slept and ate, and there were many people who enjoyed him. We were thankful God sent us to the Church of Christ in Vicksburg, Mississippi. They took very good care of us.

There was a big screen TV at the shelter. We watched the newscast whenever it came on. More than once, we saw people crying. They had just learned they had lost everything. The lucky ones like us found out that DeQuincy did not take the main hit. After a few days, we decided to head for home. Jennifer was feeling better and the decision was made. We packed everything up, including the dog and cat, and said our goodbyes. A picture of the ladies who volunteered at the shelter was taken with baby Connor. What stories we would have to tell.

The first thing we had to find was gas. To get back to DeQuincy we had to go through towns that had damage and were without electricity. The traffic was almost as bad going back as it was coming. This time nothing was open. Each town was like a ghost town. No gas stations, no restaurants, no food and no water. We were blessed to have full gas tanks and food to eat, and we rationed the water.

Stops had to be made to feed Connor. Empty parking lots away from traffic were used. More than once, bushes along a field were used for bathroom stops. When

Weather

we made it to DeQuincy, our gas tank was on empty, and we were running on fumes. We were glad to see electricity was on and a gas station was open.

God had brought us home safely.

*****

Snowstorms.

I cannot even count the snowstorms I have been through in my lifetime. As a child, I remember one storm the snow was over our white picket fence. The phone lines hanging from pole to pole were lying on top of the snow. As a child of eight, it was over my head. I could not understand why Mother would not let us outside to play in all that wonderful snow. All she said was, "We would lose you in the snow and not find you until spring." Of course, the neighbour's kids could do all kinds of things I was never allowed to do. Sure enough, there they were messing up the beautiful snow in my yard. I remember thinking, "Maybe we will not find you guys until spring."

I love snowstorms. It is a time when everything around you shuts down and stops. No traffic on the roadways to hear. No appointments to keep. For twelve to twenty-four hours, everything is quiet. The morning after the storm, there are blue skies and white snow sparkling like diamonds everywhere you look. Everything looks so clean and fresh. You want to grab a camera to take pictures of the trees, bushes, and hillsides dressed in beauty. The camera cannot capture the real beauty of what your eyes see around you.

The longest snowstorm took place in Pittsburgh, Pennsylvania. It was a March storm. Paul and I had shipped the children to a dear friend's home for Friday and Saturday. It was our wedding anniversary and we were to stay at a very nice hotel. It was snowing when we arrived, but we were told that was not the blizzard that was expected to come in. The blizzard did not start until Saturday morning, when we already had three inches of snow on the ground.

We barely made it back to our house. We had to make a 'run for it' to get the car into our driveway and off the road. The snow was so deep that we could not reach the garage. Then it snowed all of Saturday and Sunday. It was very strange for Paul and I were alone. The storm was so bad we could not collect the children. After a phone call, we were told not to worry about the kids; they were safe.

It was not until sometime on Monday we began the chore of digging out. We went into the garage, opened the garage door, and found a wall of snow in front of us. I had never seen anything like it. Three or four inches from the top, you could see daylight. At least six feet of snow was in front of us. Six feet of solid snow covering the distance between our garage and the road.

Weather

How do you shovel snow that is way above your head? Then what do you do with the snow, fill up your garage? Looking out the back door of the garage, we could see the wind had blown the snow away from the door. So we stood on chairs filled our shovels with snow and threw it out the back door.

Tuesday we still had not gotten out of the driveway and reached the road. You could only shovel snow for so long and you had to take a break and rest.

Wednesday came; watching the news on TV revealed that most roads were still not passable. It was too quiet around our house. We missed our kids. We found out a road was passable; we jumped in the car for the thirty-minute trip to pick up our children. It was dark and not too many people were on the road. Something seemed odd – not quite right. There was a road barrier separating the oncoming traffic. All of a sudden, I realized there was no other side of the road. Just a prairie of snow as far as you could see. It turned out the snowplow could not clear the snow; it was too deep. The state was waiting for a huge snow blower to come in and clear the road. We thought, "Great, we are going to pick up the kids, but how are we going to get home?" Lucky for us, the local people knew of another way back. We arrived home late. I am not sure the kids thought it was great being home. They had a blast at our friends' home. It is no wonder for our friends had five children. Two more and no one seemed to notice. Jennifer and Christopher remember this snowstorm well.

Just recently, living in Covington, Indiana, we had a snow, ice mix of a storm. It looked like a regular six to eight-inch snowfall on the ground. However, when you got closer, you found out it was as hard as a rock. Shovels were of no use. People whose cars were ready to be dug out had quite a dilemma on their hands. The white ice was so thick on the windows that they could not break it off. In addition, the tires were frozen solid to the ground.

Paul said, "Forget it." He threw sand on top and we walked elevated for three weeks or more. Some people thought putting hot water on the car windshield would take care of the problem. ("Not a good idea," says my mother) for the glass shattered. Others used picks to break the ice off their driveways and walkways. Not a good idea, so they found out a month later. The picks may have broken up the ice but also cracked and pitted their concrete. A very hard lesson to learn.

In addition, those covered rain gutters that are very popular to keep the leaves out are not good for an ice storm. They filled up with ice, and when the melting began, the water had nowhere to go but inside the house. Water damage on walls and ceilings of your nice house. The winter of 2011 was long and expensive for many in Indiana.

*****

Jesus tells more than one story about weather. One day Jesus watched as His disciples were in a boat straining at the oars, because the wind was against them. He decided to go help, but He went in a very unorthodox way. He walked to them on the water. When His disciples saw him coming walking towards them, they almost jumped out of their skin.

You cannot blame them really. If you saw someone walking towards you out of a storm, you would jump out of your skin as well. They thought Jesus was a ghost.

Jesus, seeing their reaction, how they were crying out and he saw them terrified, he spoke out to them. "Take courage, it is I. Don't be afraid." Then he climbed into the boat with them, and the wind died down, and immediately the boat reached the shore where they were headed.

Amazing, Jesus had more power than the storm.
I like a good storm. The power that God gave nature is overwhelming at times. And, yes, those cracks of thunder that are so loud it makes you jump, and at times even run. Like the time lightning hit the tree beside our house in Covington. It was like a cannon shot. It might as well have been, for it killed the tree, four computers, and the church's copying machine. Now that is power.

Maybe I like a good storm because it is a reminder to me who is in charge. God! There is nothing we can do; the lightning will hit where it will. It makes you feel small, tiny and insignificant, compared to the rest of God's creation. Still, God is there with you.

Next time you are in a storm let it remind you to focus on the Creator. All the stress and busywork that this world consumes us with, the storm will get your attention to focus more on Him and less on ourselves.

Weather

Dear God

How powerful You are! We get just a glimpse of it watching a storm. You are the creator of everything including storms.

God, I know You do not send storms to punish. Storms are a part of Your creation, just as the sun rises and sets, just as the rain falls and plants grow. Storms are part of the scheme of things.

I pray for us – who are also part of the creation. I pray that You will keep us safe in all the storms. I pray we will learn how to live among the great storms that fall on this earth.

Help us to understand and not fear storms. For we know You are with us.

We glorify You because of Your awesome power and great love.

Thank You for being my God and my Father.

In Your Son's Name, I pray.

Catherine Wilcoxson

Open Doors and Open Windows: Journey with God

**Michael and Jennifer
Christopher and Kayla**

CHAPTER 11 WEDDINGS

Has anyone ever said to you, "I have good news and bad news, what do you want to hear first?"

I love weddings. Every little girl dreams about weddings. The knight in shining armour rides up on his white stead and lifts her off her feet. She is then taken away and lives happily ever after.

When Jennifer and Michael announced the date of their wedding, I was thrilled. My mind started turning; now I can plan a wedding. I am told that, when a mother has a small wedding herself, she develops an overwhelming urge to plan a large wedding for her daughter.

I did not want a large wedding, and it was not hard to convince Paul either. I have the fondest memories of my wedding. Looking back, I would not change a thing. However, my daughter is getting married and I have this desire to make it the best wedding ever. Did you notice that Jennifer is not even in the picture yet? Since it is to be her wedding, we did sit down and make plans. My daughter was wonderful; she was perfectly willing to allow me to help her plan her wedding. I would suggest several things and she would pick what she liked best. For example, Jennifer and Michael could sing. I suggested they sing their own wedding music. Not in person, I wanted them to enjoy their wedding day, and not be nervous about singing. We recorded the music. They did a beautiful job, and to this day I have a CD I can play, which puts me right back to the day. Great memories.

We did not know what to use for the recession. Since Jennifer and I were born in Nova Scotia, and my mother, who was from Nova Scotia, was to be there, why not use bagpipes? Jennifer also graduated from High School with "Scotland of the Brave" in Pittsburgh. At Ohio Valley College the bagpipes continued with "The Fighting Scotts". We could not find anyone who could play the bagpipes in Louisiana so we used a recording. Everyone was surprised when music of the pipes sounded.

Let me paint the picture for you. We lived in Louisiana at the time. Jennifer met Michael at Ohio Valley College in West Virginia. They were not the best of students. In fact, they flunked out. Mom and Dad insisted their daughter come home. She never lived in Louisiana but we did. Home is where we were. She agreed to come home

Weddings

only if Michael could come too. They had just become engaged.

What were a Mom and Dad to do? Pray! Pray! Pray!

We agreed to Jennifer's conditions. Paul and Christopher actually made a bed out of leftover boards, bought a cheap mattress to put on it and placed it in Christopher's bedroom. Michael and Christopher would bunk together.

Jennifer and Michael both got jobs. Jennifer was the lifeguard at DeQuincy's pool. Michael was testing the waters of the job market in the area. We had five months until the wedding. Not everyone has the opportunity to get to know his or her son-in-law-to-be so well before the wedding. Michael was a little rough around the edges, but Paul took the time to guide him just as if he were our own son. Christopher and he became best friends. Michael blossomed into the wonderful person he is today.

August 15, 1998, we woke up to heavy rain, the wedding day. Rain or no rain, this is going to be a great day. Planning and preparations are done. This is the day to enjoy and remember. We had an enjoyable rehearsal dinner at our home the night before. If it is any indication, the wedding will go well.

Our house is filled with guests. My mother, Doris, has come from Nova Scotia. She has been here for over a week helping with all the preparations. Paul's mother,

Dorothy, and brother, Russell, from Nashville, and Michael's mother Maria and sister Caitlin from New Jersey are here.

Our sweet neighbors, Polly and John Miller, live in a southern home next to ours. It has the white pillars and beautiful old live oak trees famous in Louisiana in the yard. It looks like a picture out of "Gone with the Wind." Polly has offered her second floor to accommodate some of our guests. Four bedrooms, with atmosphere you could not buy. Michael the groom, Bryan his best man from Ohio, Christopher and Steven, the ushers, and Russell, are staying there. We are also using Michael and Jennifer's rented house adjoining our backyard. Jennifer and Caitlin are sleeping there.

The whole congregation is turning out for the wedding. They have not known us very long, but they are there to support us. They know Jennifer and Michael even less, but they have surrounded these young people with love and have made them part of their family. The ladies of the congregation are giving Jennifer the wedding reception for their wedding gift. We made the list of things we wanted and they provided it. Not only did they provide it, they wanted to make sure it was done the way Jennifer wanted it. Jennifer, being raised in the north, wanted her wedding according to the traditions there. Gerald, a good

Weddings

friend of ours said, "If you want a northern wedding, we will put the air conditioner down to 50 degrees."

Earlier, the church had a beautiful wedding shower for Jennifer. These things were all done with such love that it made us all feel like we belonged. We have never been treated like this before.

The wedding party is ready to leave for the church building. The sun has come out, the grandmothers and Maria, Michael's mother, have just left for the church building. Paul is here with his daughter. What a sight! Paul is wearing a tuxedo, and he is accompanying Jennifer in her beautiful wedding gown, while she pins a boutonniere to his lapel. The bridesmaids and flower girl are just beautiful. I am wearing white, which reminds me of my wedding. Here I am ready to go to my daughter's wedding. Life is full of wonderful events, and this has to be one of the best.

Christopher is walking me up the aisle; I am to light the unity candle. It is a symbol to show the beginning of a new family. Looking towards the back of the church building, I see Jennifer and her father standing there ready to walk up the aisle. I will treasure this vision of my beautiful daughter, Jennifer, and her father, my mate, in my heart forever. Paul will walk his daughter up the aisle, turn around, and perform the ceremony.

The ceremony is over.I hear the words, "I now present to you for the first time Mr. and Mrs. Michael

Boyle." The church is filled with bagpipe music. Everything went so well. What a beautiful wedding. Jennifer and Michael look so happy and love glows in their eyes. I pray they will have a marriage like Paul and I have, one that is full of happiness and is strong because we depend upon God and each other when times are hard. There will be happy times and maybe not so happy times. Either way, if they both depend upon God, everything will turn out well.

    The people who attended enjoyed the "northern" wedding reception. In days gone by, notes of well wishes and "congratulations" were sent by telegraph to the bride and groom. Today, they come by e-mail and telephone. The following are a few messages that we received:

From Paul's brother Robert, August 10, 1998, "Just a note to say may The Lord bless all of you this week. May he bless this special time in the life of all of you, may he bless the union of these his children, and they bring him much honor and glory. And may he guide and direct their path and they live long and prosper. Sort of a prayer and a blessing wish for all of you. I will be thinking of you and my heart will be with all of you. Bob"

From Lucas Kai, a friend of Catherine's from high school, dated July 25, 1998.

> *Dear Paul and Cathy,*
>
> *Best wishes to the beautiful couple and you! Those lovely pictures remind me of a Chinese saying! Let's hold hands together (guiding, supporting and loving each other every step of our life journey), let's grow old together! (Age and share the joy and endure the pain together as one)!*
>
> *God bless,*
> *Love Lucas*

Another message arrived from Catherine's sister Lois and her husband Keith:

> *PLEASE READ THE FOLLOWING MESSAGE DURING THE WEDDING RECEPTION:*
>
> *Dear Jennifer and Michael:*
> *Love and warm wishes on this the day you declare your love and commitment to each other. I know your dad, mom is especially*

proud of you, Jennifer, Uncle Keith, and I would have loved to see your dad perform your special wedding ceremony. Michael, I know your new family, Keith, will warmly welcome you and I hope to meet our new nephew someday soon.

Enjoy your wedding day, we wish you many, many happy years together. May you grow in love and understanding for each other. May God be with you and bless you!

All our love,

Aunt Lois and Uncle Keith

Regina, Canada"

The bride and groom are running towards their car through a storm of birdseed. They are wearing tee shirts, and on the front is written "Michael and Jennifer" on the back is written "Just Married."

We return home and enjoy our guests for another evening. However, something is different; another chapter has turned in our life. Life, this wonderful Life. We are surrounded with the love of God, the love of family, the love of brethren. What else can we ask for?

Weddings

The days that followed the wedding, we enjoyed spending time with my mother. We had a longer than normal visit because Air Canada was on strike. During her visit, we had the opportunity to share the Gospel of Jesus Christ with Mom, and she was baptized into Jesus Christ. The congregation at DeQuincy and our family had another time for celebration.

Fast forward to December 2004. Paul and I were living in California. We had been there less than six months. Already there were signs of stress, and we questioned what we had gotten ourselves into. God was teaching me another lesson. I was trying to learn quickly.

Christopher was attending Abilene Christian University in Texas. He would graduate the following spring. He and Kayla Dooley were planning a wedding on December 18, 2004. Afterward, they planned to return to ACU as married students.

We knew the plans of the wedding before moving to California. Part of the package before starting work with the church was to attend both Christopher's wedding in December and his graduation the following spring. It was a good thing we had the package in writing, because I am not sure the elders would have given us the time off to attend our son's wedding.

The wedding was to be held in Atlanta, Georgia. We flew in and arrived a few days before the wedding.

Jennifer, Michael, Logan, and baby Ethan joined us from Louisiana. We shared a suite at the hotel, and it was so good to see them. It broke our hearts to have to leave them and go to California. We were all together again, even if it was for a very short time.

Paul and I helped decorate for the wedding. That evening we had a rehearsal dinner. Planning a rehearsal dinner was very difficult living in California. Kayla picked her favorite restaurant, and we had a family gathering the night before the wedding, her family and ours.

A beautiful Christmas wedding. A forest of decorated Christmas trees was at the front. Christopher standing beside his father watched his bride come to him. Paul was thrilled to perform the wedding ceremony. Jennifer was a bridesmaid wearing a beautiful cranberry red dress. Michael was the best man and Logan, who was three years old, threw red rose petals leading the way for Kayla, the beautiful bride. There were others in the wedding party, including, Kayla's sister Megan, who was the maid of honor and another boy younger than Logan helped throw the rose petals. The boys were dressed in golden suits with short pants. The younger boy ran straight up the aisle towards his mother. Logan was very proud of the job he was asked to do, and slowly marched up that aisle carefully, dropping each petal as he went. Nannie was so proud. I was totally focused on watching my children.

Weddings

Kayla and Christopher left among fireworks sparklers. Kayla was still wearing her beautiful wedding gown. Her gown was covered with a dark velvet cape. She looked like a princess indeed. I expected to see a white stead waiting for the prince and princess in the parking lot. However, Christopher helped his bride inside a car with signs of "Just Married" and cans tied to the back.

It was over – saying goodbye to Jennifer, Michael, Logan, and baby Ethan was the saddest thing. They were off to the airport and on their way back to Louisiana. I did not know when I would see them again.

Paul and I decided that since we were on the East Coast we would fly to Nova Scotia for Christmas. It was the first time I was home for Christmas in over twenty years. Christmas was held at my sister Lois's home. It snowed! We had not seen snow in ten years.

The new year 2005 and we arrived back in California. The elders were not pleased we went to Nova Scotia for Christmas. "Who said you could go there?"

We were quite surprised and answered, "It was in the "package" when we agreed to come here." It was not as if we secretly went away. It was there in black and white for all to see, and it had been agreed to. The "package" did not mean much to these elders, for they changed everything that was in it.

I have one more wedding story to tell. As you can imagine we have been involved with many weddings over 35 years. The wedding I am about to tell of is the most unusual experience we have ever had. It needs to be written down.

The wedding plans seemed to take place like any other wedding. Paul did the pre-marital counseling and the wedding date was chosen. The problems started the night before the wedding during the rehearsal. The parents and flower girl were not present.

The following morning we got this strange phone call from the photographer. He wanted to check out the address for the wedding reception. We gave it to him. He said we have a big problem. This wedding has two different locations for the reception, and no one is around at the bride's home to take pre-wedding pictures.

When we got to the church, we found a wedding gown hanging in the fellowship hall. No one, including the groom or groom's family, knew where the bride was. Guests started to arrive. The church was decorated; music was playing, but not a sign of the bride.

Time came to begin, still no bride. One half hour went by, still no bride. I am in the back trying to keep the groom and his mother calm. "Don't worry," I said. "We don't even have to make an announcement to your guests until the bride is over an hour late." I do not know where I

Weddings

came up with that, but it sounded good. The groom's mother relaxed, even if it was just a little.

The hour went by, still no bride. The guests were getting very anxious. Our Jennifer was to sing a solo, so I sent her up front to do her duty. Two hours after the time the wedding was to start, and just before Paul was to make some kind of announcement, a car sped into the parking lot. Out jumped the bride carrying a wedding gown. Now we have two wedding gowns.

I remember saying, "I will take care of this!" I ran to the car and she fell into my arms crying. I took her into Paul's office and told her everything was going to be fine. Then her story came tumbling out. Her mother had stolen her wedding gown the night before, and would not give it to her. Her mother did not want the wedding to take place, for the groom was not Catholic.

The bride woke up early on her wedding day and bought a new wedding gown. Then she found out her father would not give her away. Her sister would not stand with her, nor would she allow her young daughter to be flower girl. You can imagine the commotion going on at the bride's house.

Finally, just as the wedding was supposed to start, the bride decided to stand up to everyone in her family. She managed to find her wedding dress and here she was. Here was a young woman in her late twenties sitting before me crushed.

"Do you want to marry this man?"

"Yes, of course, I do," was the answer.

"Fine, let's make it happen. Would you like to have Robert Smith walk you down the aisle?" I knew they were friends. Robert was one of the leaders in the church and I knew he was sitting upstairs.

"Yes, that would be good."

"I also saw Susan, a five-year-old dressed in the prettiest dress. Would you like Susan to be your flower girl?"

"Yes, but don't you think this is short notice."

"You let me take care of everything. You sit here and calm yourself. I will be right back with Robert."

I remember walking through the gathering of the groom's family. "Everything is just fine," I said as I walked by. Then I walked up the aisle of the church, tapped Robert on the shoulder, and said, "You are needed downstairs."

Robert took time to talk to the bride. He told her it would be a privilege and a great honor to walk her down the aisle. Meantime, I had Susan and her mother at the back of the church. We now were ready for a wedding. Almost three hours late, but we had a wedding.

The bride enjoyed the wedding reception. The reception she had planned. We sent them on their way.

Weddings

Later, I was told she did not even have time to pack for the honeymoon. However, someone else took care of that.

*****

Yes, I love weddings. What I do not like is the trend that brides think more of their weddings, spending great amounts of money, than they do of their marriage. We know the divorce rate is very high. Divorce is an awful thing, for you know how I feel about that subject from reading a previous chapter.

*****

I believe that Jesus liked weddings. Whether it was planned by Him or not, His first miracle took place at a wedding. Jesus was at Bethany with John the Baptist. Jesus was baptized and John said, "I saw the Spirit come down from heaven as a dove and remain on him." And he heard a voice say, "This is my Son in whom I am pleased."

The next day Jesus spent it with Andrew and Peter at their home. The day after this Jesus left Galilee and found two more of his apostles. And on the third day, there was a wedding.

> On the third day, a wedding took place at Cana in Galilee. Jesus mother was there, and Jesus and his disciples had also been invited to the wedding. When the wine was gone, Jesus' mother said to him. "They have no more wine."

"Dear woman, why do you involve me?" Jesus replied. "My time has not yet come."

His mother said to the servants, "Do whatever he tells you."

Nearby stood six stone water jars, the kind used by the Jews for ceremonial washing, each holding from twenty to thirty gallons.

Jesus said to the servants, "Fill the jars with water," so they filled them to the brim.

Then he told them, "Now draw some out and take it to the master of the banquet."

They did so, and the master of the banquet tasted the water that had been turned into wine. He did not realize where it had come from, though the servants who had drawn the water knew. Then he called the bridegroom aside and said, "Everyone brings out the choice wine first and then the cheaper wine after the guests have had too much to drink; but you have saved the best till now. This the first of his miraculous signs, Jesus performed at Cana in Galilee. He thus revealed his glory and his disciples put their faith in him." [32]

Weddings

Weddings are special times, times of new beginnings. We enjoyed our wedding and the wedding ceremonies Paul has performed throughout his ministry. We pray for all those he has joined together in the sight of God.

Dear God:

Thank you for Jennifer and Christopher. Years have passed and they are n longer children. Watch over them as they live their lives for You. Protect them in this world.

Be with them both, as they have families of their own.

Help Jennifer be a good mother for Logan, Ethan, and Connor.

Help Christopher to be a kind and loving husband and a great father to Lily.

Help Paul and me to support them in all they do.

We love them, Father, as we know You love us.

We pray this in Your Son's name.
Paul and Catherine Wilcoxson

**This Open Gate Reminds Me
Of The Open Gate Of Heaven**

CHAPTER 12 FUNERALS

Now for the Bad News!

We are all going to die. All of us. It does not matter how old you are or how healthy you are, we are all going to die. All of us will have that appointment to keep. It is just that we do not know when.

Death scares people, and for good reason. Anyone who has experienced losing a loved one will tell you it hurts right down to the depth of your soul. It takes years, and some people never get over the death of a loved one.

The year was 1996. Paul and I were working with the church in Maryland. The church was planning a special event, a special service, and dinner inviting the whole neighbourhood, including the mayor and other government dignitaries of the town. Planning meetings had taken place; decorations had been made and were ready.

Less than one week before the great event, I received a phone call from Nova Scotia. My father was dying and I needed to come home. My dad had been in bad health for many years. However, it is very hard to receive a phone call like that. My dad Elbridge Reginald Kenney died that night.

Paul could not leave. You cannot just cancel a special event like the one planned. Paul and I decided that I would fly home by myself. My lonely trip home allowed time to ponder many things. I spent ten days with my family in Nova Scotia. I had not been home in several years. The last time was the funeral of my sister, Marlane. Do I only go home to bury loved ones? It was a time of excitement of seeing my family again. But I would be brought back to reality. My dad was not there to see. The most vivid memory that I would have of that trip is the funeral and the lonely cemetery by the Atlantic Ocean. When we arrived there was a "piper" standing before the many graves. He wore a kilt and was playing "Amazing Grace" on his bagpipes. The weather was cold, the sun was shining, and you could see the effect of the wind making white caps on the bright blue ocean. I was thankful I got to say goodbye. For that is what death is, the final goodbye.

*****

In the same cemetery in Nova Scotia sixty years earlier in 1917, Heman Godfrey Kenney, Elbridge's grandfather proceeded him in the final goodbye. The advents of the day are similar, for funerals take on the sameness.

In the same cemetery in Nova Scotia sixty years earlier in 1917, Heman Godfrey Kenney, Elbridge's grandfather proceeded him in the final goodbye. The advents of the day are similar, for funerals take on the sameness.

The following account is taken from my book, The Adventures of Captain Heman Kenney and Lady Catherine 1833-1917.

> The death of Alexander's father, Heman, was very hard on him. Alexander, (Alexander is Elbridge's father) spent all his free time sitting with his father those last years. When Heman was well enough, Alexander asked him to share stories of the adventures he had with *Lady Catherine,* Heman's schooner.
>
> Elizabeth, Heman's wife, continued to look out the window at the lighthouse. As the years passed, the pain grew bearable. Now, as she thought back to that day, she knew Heman would smile just knowing how many

people cared for him. She closed her eyes and her mind took her back . . . .

Two black horses with red feathered plumbs fastened to their heads, pulled the hearse carriage up the lane way. Swallows flew in and out of the doors of the barn as they passed by. The undertaker, Mr. Webb, brought them to a stop, between the well and the front door of the blue-gray-shingled cottage. The family was gathered in the kitchen and dining room area. Final goodbyes were completed.

"Are you ready?" Mr. Webb asked the question to a group of men sitting on one side of the dining room. Captain Kenney's crew was all present: Henry, Patrick, Moses, John Charles and Dick, dressed in their green jackets and green vests. This would be the last time they would honor their Captain.

Henry, being the first mate, stepped forward, "We are ready."

"Mrs. Kenney?"

"She is in with the Captain." Henry led the way to the small living room.

Funerals

"Are you ready, Mrs. Kenney?" Mr. Webb was trying to do his job. Elizabeth looked up at the two men.

"Elizabeth looks so frail," thought Henry.

"Where is Alexander?" she asked.

"He is in his room," answered Henry.

"Please summon him, Henry." She turned to Mr. Webb, "Please, I need a few more minutes."

"Certainly." The undertaker left her alone with Heman.

Alexander entered the room and sat in a chair. It was not close to his mother, nor was it close to his father. "Come beside me, Alexander."

"I'd rather not," Alexander replied.

Elizabeth looked upon her son, "Please, Alexander, do it for me." Alexander would do anything for his mother, but she was asking something of him that was hard to give.

"Be strong, Alexander."

"That's what Father always said," Alexander cried. "But I could never be as strong as he was." He raised himself to his feet and slowly walked to her side.

Elizabeth took his hand as if he were a child. "Your father loved you, Alexander."

"Mother, what will we do without him?" Finally, tears came to the surface of his eyes.

"I've asked the same thing, my son. You will be the leader of this family now. This will be your house. The Kenneys will continue to make some kind of mark in this community.

Mr. Webb was at the door, "Mrs. Kenney, I hate to interrupt, but it is time. Are you ready?"

Elizabeth looked towards Alexander. He nodded his head; he was ready. She then looked over towards Heman lying in the rough wooden coffin. She walked towards him, lifted his hand to her lips for a final farewell. She turned to Mr. Webb, "Yes, Heman is ready."

People were gathering at St. Andrew's Cemetery. One could see from this hill several schooners moored off the Watt

Section Wharf. They seemed to be circled around *Lady Catherine*, consoling her, for she was in mourning. From the top of her spar flew black flags, and her bow had black banners hanging from the side. The afternoon breezes helped them wave a goodbye. *Lady Catherine* knew her Captain's heart was no longer beating. He no longer heard the call of the sea. She was mourning her loss.

The horses, dressed in their red-feathered bridles, made their turn, rounding the well, as they headed back out the lane. Slowly, very slowly, they turned right onto the rocky road. Elizabeth wanted to walk. "Heman and I walked to the cemetery every evening when he was well. I want to walk." The whole family walked.

The procession stopped outside the Rood's gate. The Rood family was waiting. Mary Elizabeth, Eric, and their children joined the procession. Mary Elizabeth took her Mother's arm, and Alexander took her other. Together they followed the horse-drawn hearse, as it made a left-hand turn and began its slow climb up the dusty hill. As the road leveled off, they approached the cemetery, where horses and wagons were parked on both sides of the road. The iron gate was swung open. The horses slowly pulled its cargo to the top of Cemetery hill. The congregation gathered at the open-air church and stood as the family walked up the hill.

Captain Kenney's crew, dressed in green, carried the wooden casket and placed it beside a freshly dug hole. The family settled in the section reserved for them. Many of the men had to stand, for the Kenney family numbered more than twenty.

Reverend McDonald was standing to the side, speaking quietly to a Captain. Captain Woods, standing by the Reverend was heard saying, "Are you ready? It is time to sail."

The old Reverend looked up to the old Captain, cleared his voice, "With God's help I am ready." He picked up the gold cross, held it high and proceeded to the front, his white robe swishing with each step he took.

Funerals

A hush fell over the crowd. Word had spread throughout more than one community that the famous Civil War Captain had arrived the day before at Watt Section Wharf. After Reverend McDonald had finished with a prayer, Captain Woods approached the front.

"Today is a sad day for me. I have lost a great friend. My heart is heavy, but how can it compare to the breaking heart of Elizabeth, Heman's true love." He stopped for a moment looking over towards Elizabeth. She acknowledged Woods with a smile and a nod of her head. "And to Heman's children," Woods continued, "a day they have lost a great father." Soft crying could be heard. The children were not as strong as their Mother was. Elizabeth knew her time of mourning would come. Today, she would honor her husband. ". And you the community have lost a good neighbour."

Elizabeth didn't hear the rest of Captain Wood's speech. Her mind drifted off like fog rolling over the sea. She closed her eyes and saw a young girl running on *Lady Catherine's* deck, then her engagement and the trip to Ireland. Her first-born, and then the move to the great Show House, the fire, and now this. She opened her eyes to see the white caps on the deep blue ocean. *"The sea is calling, my love. Go on, for you are free to sail for eternity."* Elizabeth set his spirit free.

*****

Being a minister's wife, I have attended many funerals. Our car with Paul and me inside, have lead the hearse to many cemeteries. I took it to be my job to comfort the families, and I was good at it. I probably could get a job at a funeral home.

I remember having a conversation with a lady at her 100th birthday party. Knowing her well, I was kidding her when I asked, "How did you live for so long?"

I was surprised by her answer. "I learned to say goodbye to all those friends and family that have died before me. Catherine, if you can learn to let death go, your life will be happier for it." I am sure it is hard to do, but good advice.

*****

Funerals

Mark tells us something Jesus did while He was here amongst us.

> The synagogue ruler came to Jesus. His daughter was seriously ill. The leader must have loved his daughter and he knew his only chance was to go to Jesus. News travels quickly. When Jesus was performing miracles, the leaders knew about it. And that day He needed a miracle.
>
> While he was with Jesus, men from his household came and said, "Your daughter is dead, why bother the teacher anymore?"
>
> Ignoring what they said Jesus told the synagogue ruler, "Don't be afraid, just believe."
>
> Jesus did not allow the crowd to go with him, but Peter, James and John followed Jesus and the ruler. When they came to the home of the synagogue ruler, there was a crowd of people. They were crying and wailing loudly.
>
> Jesus went in and said to them; "Why all this commotion and wailing? The child is not dead but sleeping."

The crowd stopped crying and wailing. Now they were laughing. They were laughing at the Son of God. Have you ever been laughed at? It does not feel very good, does it?

Jesus turned around and put them all out. Can you picture that? He clears the room.

Jesus took the child's father, mother, and the disciples who were with him, and went in where the child was. Jesus took her by the hand and said, "Little girl, I say to you, get up!"

The room must have been crowded. There would have been six, including Jesus, seven when you count the dead child.

Immediately. Not ten minutes later, not two days later. Immediately the girl stood up and walked around.

Mark remembered the story so well he added that she was twelve years old.

At this, they were completely astonished.

Just think of who was astonished. I am sure the ones at the top of the list were the parents. It was a good day for them. Next in line were Peter, James, and John. Then the next on the list was the followers, the men who delivered the message to the synagogue leader. These ones said to

Funerals

give up and not bother the teacher further. For his daughter was dead. And last but not least on the list, were the guys that laughed. All of these people were completely astonished.

And Jesus ended it all by saying, "Give the girl something to eat."[33]

What was Jesus saying? Was death just no big deal to Him?

Perhaps you are saying, "Yeah, that's Jesus; He is God. Maybe He doesn't understand how much death hurts us."

*****

One of Jesus' closest friends died.

> Upon Jesus arrival, He found that Lazarus had already been in the tomb for four days.
>
> Many Jews had come to comfort Lazarus' sisters, Martha and Mary, in the loss of their brother. Martha had received news that Jesus was on his way and was just outside Bethany. She went out to meet him.
>
> "Lord," Martha said to Jesus; "if you had been here, my brother would not have died.

But I know that even now God will give you whatever you ask."

Jesus said to her, "Your brother will rise again."

Martha answered, "I know he will rise again in the resurrection at the last day."

Jesus said to her "I am the resurrection and the life. He who believes in me will live, even though he dies; and whoever lives and believes in me, will never die. Do you believe this?"

"Yes Lord." She told him, "I believe that you are the Christ, the Son of God, who was to come into the world."

Martha then went back and told Mary that Jesus was just outside of the city and asking for her. Mary quickly went to him.

When the Jews who had been with Mary in the house comforting her, noticed how quickly she got up and went out, they followed her, supposing she was going to the tomb, to mourn there. When Mary reached Jesus, she fell at his feet. She said, "If you had been here Lazarus would not have died."

Now, I want you to look closely at what happens next. **When Jesus saw her weeping and the Jews who had come along with her also weeping, He was deeply moved in spirit and troubled.**

Here it is! Yes, Jesus is God, but He is feeling, He is experiencing what you and I feel about death. He is not feeling well. He was deeply moved in Spirit – His heart was hurting and breaking. He is troubled – He is about to lose control of his feelings. He is feeling pain right down to his soul.

He tries to recover by asking a question, "Where have you laid him?"

"Come, we will show You."

Then Jesus lost control, broke down, the pain got to him.

You have been there – death will do this to everyone.

Jesus wept.

This is a nice way to put it, Jesus wept. However, Jesus cried. Maybe even sobbed. Cried to the point that the people gathered around him noticed and made a comment.

"See how he loved him."

God was in a man's body. The heart and emotions in that body broke down. He cried until he emptied His heart.

We say, "Cry – get it out – you will feel better." Jesus knows. He knows how bad it feels. Death is one of the worst things we have to deal with here on this earth. Jesus knows it hurts.

Then we have the critics.

The reason why we do not like to cry is the critics.Critical people will think we are weak. They will not understand.

> Some of the Jews whispered to each other. "Could he who opened the eyes of the blind man have kept this man from dying?"
>
> Jesus, once more deeply moved, came to the tomb. Jesus still did not have control of His emotions. The tomb was a cave with a stone laid across the entrance.
>
> "Take away the stone!"

Can you not hear the gasps coming from those standing with Him?

> "But Lord!" said Martha, "by this time there is a bad odor, for he has been there four days."

This is not what Martha expected. Everyone around Jesus thought his grief had turned him 'mad'. You just do not take away the stone. You do not go inside a tomb. Talk about being unclean. The Jews knew the priest would not even look at you.

Jesus was not 'mad'.

> He turned to Martha, "Did I not tell you that if you believed, you would see the glory of God."
> Therefore, they took away the stone.
> Jesus looked up. "Father, I thank you that you have heard me. I knew that you always hear me, but I said this for the benefit of the people standing here, that they may believe that you sent me."
> Then he said with a loud voice. "Lazarus, come out!"

And he did!

He must have been stumbling around for he had strips of linen wrapped around his feet and arms and a cloth around his face. He must have had difficulties, for Jesus said, "Take off the grave clothes and let him go."

To this very day, Jesus still knows how we feel about death. [34]

Death was the reason Jesus came to earth in the first place. Death is a separation from life to death. Sin is a death that separates man from God. God could not stand for us to be away from Him. Our Father was going to do something about it. He sent Jesus, His Son.

*****

The greatest death of all times was the day man killed God's Son.

Jesus was betrayed by a kiss, by one of his own disciples, Judas. The detachment of soldiers took Jesus away to Annas an enemy of Jesus and the father-in-law of Caiaphas the high priest. Here He was questioned. However, it did not matter how He answered; it would make no difference. He was struck in the face, and when they were finished with Him, sent to Caiaphas.

Caiaphas sent Jesus to the palace of the Roman governor, Pilate. The Jews his accusers would not enter the palace, for they would become unclean in any presence of a Roman. These Jews wanted to take part in the 'Passover' that very evening.

Pilate came out to them and asked, "What charges are you bringing against this man?"

"If he were not a criminal," they replied, "We would not have handed Him over to you."

Pilate said, "Take Him yourselves and judge Him by your own law."

"But we have no right to execute anyone."

Pilate then went back inside the palace summoned Jesus and asked him; "Are you the King of the Jews?"

"Is that your own idea?" Jesus asked, or did others talk to you about me?"

"Am I a Jew?" Pilate replied. "It was your people and your chief priest who handed you over to me. What is it you have done?"

Jesus said, "My kingdom is not of this world. If it were, my servants would fight to prevent my arrest by the Jews. But now my kingdom is from another place."

"You are a king, then!" said Pilate.

Jesus answered, "You are right in saying I am a king. In fact, for this reason I was born, and for this I came into the world, to testify to the truth. Everyone on the side of truth listens to me.

"What is truth?" Pilate asked. With this he went out again to the Jews and said, "I find no basis for a charge against him. But it is your custom for me to release to you one prisoner at the time of the Passover. Do you want me to release 'the king of the Jews'?"

They shouted back, "No not him!" Give us Barabbas." Now Barabbas had taken part in a rebellion.

Then Pilate took Jesus and had him flogged. The soldiers twisted together a crown of thorns and put it on his head. They clothed Him in a purple robe and went up to him again and again, saying, "Hail, King of the Jews!" And they struck him in the face.

Once more Pilate came out and said to the Jews, "Look, I am bringing him out to you to let you know that I find no basis for a charge against him. When Jesus came out wearing the crown of thorns and purple robe, he said, "Here is the man."

As soon as the chief priests and their officials saw him, they shouted, Crucify! Crucify!

Pilate did not want to crucify him. The Jews insisted, "We have a law, and according to that law he must die, because he claimed to be the Son of God."

When Pilate heard this, he was afraid. He asked Jesus more questions and Jesus remained quiet.

"Do you refuse to speak to me?" Pilate said. "Don't you realize I have power either to free you or crucify you?"

Jesus answered. "You would have no power over me if it were not given to you from above. Therefore the one who handed me over to you is guilty of a greater sin."

Pilate tried to let him go. But the Jews shouted "If you let this man go, you are no friend of Caesar. Anyone who claims to be a king opposes Caesar."

That is all Pilate needed was for this case to go to Caesar. He was in enough trouble with Caesar as it was. Therefore, he sent this problem case to Herod. During the time Jesus was with Herod, He remained silent. It did not take long for Herod to send Jesus back to Pilate telling him to take care of it.

Pilate brought Jesus out and sat down on the judge's seat at a place known as the

Stone Pavement. When Pilate saw that he was getting nowhere, but that instead an uproar was starting, he took water and washed his hands in front of the crowd. "I am innocent of this man's blood." He then released Barabbas to them. However, he had Jesus flogged, and handed Him over to be crucified.

The soldiers took charge of Jesus. Carrying His own cross, he went towards the place of the Skull also known as Golgotha. When He could no longer carry his cross, a man from Cyrene, named Simon was forced to carry the cross.

They crucified Him, and two others. One on each side and Jesus in the middle.

Pilate had a sign fastened to the cross. It read, "Jesus of Nazareth, The King of the Jews." It was written in Aramaic, Latin and Greek. This was for everyone to read. The chief priests protested to Pilate. "At least change the sign to say this man claimed to be king of the Jews."

Pilate answer was "What I have written, I have written."

The soldiers took Jesus' clothes, dividing them into four shares, one for each of them. There was one garment that was seamless, woven in one piece from top to bottom.

"Let us not tear it," they said to one another. "Let's decide by lot who will get it." Near the cross, stood his mother Mary and Mary Magdalene. When Jesus saw his mother and the disciple whom he loved standing nearby, He said to his mother, "Dear woman, here is your son." and to the disciple, "Here is your mother." From that time on, the disciple took her into his home.

After a time Jesus said, "I am thirsty." A jar of wine vinegar was there; it was soaked in a sponge, put on a stalk and lifted to Jesus lips. When he had received the drink, Jesus said; "It is finished." With that, He bowed his head and gave up His spirit.

The Jews did not want bodies on crosses during the Sabbath, which was the next day. They asked that the legs be broken so death would be hastened. The soldiers broke the legs of the men on either side of Jesus. However, when they came to Jesus and found that He was already dead, they did not break His legs. Instead, one of the soldiers pierced Jesus' side with a spear, bringing a sudden flow of blood and water.

These things happened so that the scripture would be fulfilled; "Not one of his bones will be broken." and "They will look on the one they have pierced."

From the sixth hour until the ninth hour, darkness came over all the land. And the moment Jesus gave up His spirit the curtain of the temple was torn in two from top to bottom. The earth shook and the rocks split. The tombs broke open and bodies of many holy people who had died were raised to life.

When the centurion and those with him who were guarding Jesus saw the earthquake and all that had happened, they were terrified and exclaimed, "Surely he was the Son of God!"

Joseph of Arimathea, who had himself become a disciple of Jesus went to Pilate and asked for Jesus' body. Pilate ordered that it be given to him. Joseph accompanied by Nicodemus, took the body, wrapped it in a clean linen cloth, and placed it in his own new tomb that he had cut out of the rock. They rolled a big stone in front of the entrance and went away.

Pilate ordered the tomb be made secure until the third day. He had been told how Jesus had said he would die and raise again in three days. He did not want the disciples to come and steal the body and tell the people that He had been raised from the dead. A seal was placed on the tomb and a guard posted.

The funeral had not taken place yet. They had to wait until after the Sabbath. Mary Magdalene, Mary the mother of Jesus and Salome brought spices so they might anoint Jesus' body.

Very early on the first day of the week, just after sunrise, they were on their way to the tomb and they asked each other "Who will roll the stone away from the tomb?"

But when they looked up, they saw that the stone had been rolled away. As they entered the tomb, they saw a young man dressed in a white robe sitting on the right side, and they were alarmed.

"Don't be alarmed." he said, "You are looking for Jesus the Nazarene, who was crucified. He has risen! He is not here. See the place where they laid him."

"Go tell his disciples. He has risen!"[35]

Death could not keep Him! Jesus conquered death and said:

"I am the one who was dead but I am alive for evermore and have the keys to death and Hades."[36]

Jesus is the ultimate funeral crasher. He crashed His own funeral.

Jesus had victory over death and we too can have the same victory through Jesus. He has overcome the world. We can too.

I write these things to you who believe in the name of the Son of God so that you may know that you have eternal life. This is the confidence we have in approaching God; that if we ask anything according to his will, he hears us. And if we know that he hears us –

whatever we ask – we know that we have what we asked of him. [37]

"Death has been swallowed up in victory. Where, O death, is your victory? Where, O death, is your sting." The sting of death is sin, and the power of sin is the law. But thanks be to God! He gives us the victory through our Lord Jesus Christ.[38]

Dear God:

Thank You for Your Son, Jesus. Your only Son, whom You sent to this earth for me, to die on that cross as my sacrifice, to forgive me of my sins. Dying on the cross was the bad news. The good news is He left that tomb and conquered death. How can I ever thank You enough for such a gift?

Your Son was the ultimate funeral crasher. He crashed His own funeral

Just to know, Jesus knows, how I feel when death invades my life makes it a little easier to walk through the valley of death.

There is no death in heaven. No pain felt to one's soul. Until I get there, help me deal with the pain of death here on earth. Comfort me, put Your arms around me, carry me. Let me feel Your love and Your presence all around me.

Thank You for life. Help me to live for You.

I pray in Your Son's name.
Jesus, man's Savior
Catherine Wilcoxson

Whitehall Church of Christ Building
WHITEHALL BOROUGH, PITTSBURGH,
PENNSYLVANIA

CHAPTER 13 TRADITIONS

Tradition is "an inherited established or customary pattern of thought, action or behavior."

We all have traditions. New traditions and old, we like to know what direction our lives are going in. To practice familiar traditions gives us great comfort.

I was talking to my son Christopher the other day. I asked him what traditions we had living in Pittsburgh, Pennsylvania. It did not take him long to give me a whole list.

Every Memorial Day we would pack up the camper and head to Raccoon Creek State Park. The day marked the opening day of the camping season. We never missed a year. Nine years straight while living in Pittsburgh, Jennifer and Christopher knew this would take place and they loved it.

Christopher learned to ride a bicycle, and Jennifer learned to be a leader. She was in charge of setting up camp. We had a small camper, so Jennifer and Christopher pitched a tent where they really experienced camping. To this day Jennifer can put up a tent better than anyone I have ever seen. She does not even need the instructions.

Another springtime tradition was softball season for Jennifer. For nine years, we enjoyed watching Jennifer play catcher, third base, shortstop and first base. We attended softball games in the cold, in the early spring, in the heat of summer, and even in the rain. We loved every minute.

Back to Christopher's list. When school was out for the summer, the trips to the Baldwin Public Pool began. The pool was on the other side of Baldwin Borough. We lived in boroughs in Pittsburgh. Almost daily Patti and I would trek Jennifer, Christopher and Sarah to the pool.

Camp Concern came up every July. Camp Concern, a church camp, took place at Raccoon Creek State Park in their wilderness campground. We attended during Junior Week. Paul and I taught Bible. I remember the inner city kids the most. One year stands out in my memory, when I was assigned to several girls from the inner city of Pittsburgh. When they arrived on Sunday afternoon, they made quite an entrance. As friends of mine dropped off their kids, I remember them saying, "Poor Catherine, I wouldn't want to be in her shoes this week."

Traditions

"Have no fear," I replied. "Don't worry for me, for it will not be as hard as you may think." What my friends did not know and what I had already experienced from years past is that these city kids were completely out of their element. I said, "Just wait until the sun goes down and darkness falls and their toughness will melt like butter."

Just think about it. These children might have seen trees lining the streets, but they have never been in a forest. These children have never seen darkness. Downtown Pittsburgh is lit up like a Christmas tree at all times, and they have never heard quiet. The absence of noise can be quite frightening when you are used to hearing it around you day and night.

I gathered my chicks around me, several young ladies, and directed them to the cabin they would call home for one week. They were not impressed. I was not either, but that is another story. The cabin had bare rafters and unfinished walls. There were holes in the walls where the knots of the wood had fallen out. Several metal cots with thin mattresses were against the walls, waiting for blankets and a pillow. So far, I did not have happy campers.

I left them to set up their house. "If you need me, I will be in my cabin," I said, as I pointed to one of a dozen cabins that made up the girls' village.

"We don't need you," they said when I left.

I just smiled. "Be at the 'mess hall' at 6 p.m., and, do not be late."

Everyone knew about my group of ladies before the day was over, for their behavior made sure of that. Then it got dark. Even though I warned them to bring a flashlight with them, they did not. When it was time to walk back to the girls' village through the forest, their toughness melted quickly. They could not even see the pathway, for the forest closes in on you in the dark. Here I was with several young ladies to lead back to our village and only one flashlight, mine. "Okay, let's go and I started walking. I did not even have to look behind me, for I knew they did not want to be left behind. I looked like a mother duck with her babies following close behind. They were sticking to me like glue.

The cabins only had one light bulb. This of course sent shadows around the room. Insects that had been swept out of their home during the day, where now trying to reclaim it back at night. We had bats. Now the girls knew why I had a tennis racket and a net. Because these girls were completely out of their tough world, I was able to have wonderful times to teach them that they had other choices in their future and their lives. I taught them the love of God and that He cared for each one of them. I must admit I did have to threaten to take away their light bulb more than once that week.

Traditions

My kids loved Camp Concern. Christopher was only four years old the first time he spent a week in the boys' village with his dad. Christopher was awarded camper of the week, when he was old enough to be a camper. Jennifer became a counselor. She was good at it and was assigned the more difficult children. Me, I still wonder how I survived those cabins, with the mice, bugs and bats. I prayed for the kids that had to go back to a difficult life. We had them for one week; I pray we made a difference.

*****

Our family loved living in Pittsburgh. Pittsburgh is famous for Heinz Ketchup, Clark Bars, Klondikes, and bridges over rivers, football, lots of hills and inclines. The city has three rivers downtown, the Monongahela, the Ohio and Allegany. Oh, yeah, not to forget, "Eat 'n Park".

Everyone in Pittsburgh is a fan of the 'Steelers" and own a 'terrible towel'. Sunday when the Steelers are playing, the city streets are empty as well as the malls. Everyone is home watching the game.

There are many ethnic neighborhoods in the city. The North Side is German. Here you will find German food and the Steelers' Stadium and football. The South Side along the Monongahela River there are Ukrainian, Serbian, and Lithuanian neighborhoods. Ethnic food like Kielbasa and porgies are sold in small grocery and specialty stores.

Squirrel Hill is Jewish culture. A part of Christopher was left here. He won an award for writing a poem about the holocaust. His poem is in the Jewish museum in Squirrel Hill. You can find good food in Squirrel Hill, especially in the kosher deli and staples such as chicken soup with Matzah balls or bagels and lox.

Bloomfield sits on a high plateau overlooking the strip district and downtown. This is the Italian heritage with music, festivals and song. Paul and I would like to go to the Strip district (It is not what you may think) every Saturday morning. Here booths and stores open selling fresh vegetables, fish, meat and anything else you may think of. We never came home hungry, for we always found something good to eat.

To this day, we have great friends who live in Pittsburgh. Friends and fond memories.

*****

Many traditions of Vacation Bible Schools, traveling to many youth rallies, and serving people are just a part of who the Wilcoxsons are. We also had times when we visited family. For some reason God asked us to serve Him in places where we were far away from family. It continues today, and a long time ago, I made a promise to God that I would go wherever He needed me to go. He held me to that promise. That did not mean we forgot about family. Trips made to visit Grandma and Uncle Russell and Aunt Olene,

Traditions

and cousins in Nashville always were a big part of our lives.

In addition, of course, special trips back to Nova Scotia to visit my family, Nanna and Papa and lots of aunts and uncles and cousins. Paul promised me when he took me away from Nova Scotia that he would bring me back every two years. That is a big tradition that I like to keep.

The traditions I grew up with will always remain with me. One being Thanksgiving. Thanksgiving in Canada is the second Monday in October. October is when the harvest is gathered before the first frost. Thanksgiving is a day to be thankful you have gathered enough food to endure the long winter.

November 11th is Remembrance Day. The whole country takes this day to remember the brave men and woman for the courage and devotion in the face of extreme hardships. Thousands of Canadian's and probably many more than that, wear red poppies for the first 11 days of November. Poppies can be bought everywhere. You just pick up a poppy and place your money in the box, whatever you wish to give. A lot of Loonies and Toonies[39] are collected. The money helps those who are in the armed forces.

This tradition has a double meaning for our family. It also was my father's birthday. Elbridge Kenney was born November 11, 1914. In our house, we had a birthday party.

My dad was lucky to have his birthday off from work every year.

Birthday parties were a big thing in our family. Mother, was trained to be a cook for the officers in the World War II. She knew how to decorate everything, including our birthday cakes. She baked a sponge cake and when it was decorated, it looked professionally done. This was before the trend to take classes on how to decorate a cake. Birthdays were the only times we had pop in the house, well, birthdays and Christmas. We had orange flavor, Sprite and ginger ale. Three large bottles did not last long with a family of eight.

*****

Many traditions of Vacation Bible Schools, traveling to many youth rallies, and serving people are just a part of who the Wilcoxsons are. We also had times when we visited family. For some reason God asked us to serve Him in places where we were far away from family. It continues today, and a long time ago, I made a promise to God that I would go wherever He needed me to go. He held me to that promise. That did not mean we forgot about family. Trips made to visit Grandma and Uncle Russell and Aunt Olene, and cousins in Nashville always were a big part of our lives.

*****

If you want to talk about traditions, Louisiana is your place. They have more holidays and more traditions than any

Traditions

other does. You may think you have left the country when you move to Louisiana. I remember asking Mary, "How in the world am I, a girl from Canada, going to be able to live here?

She answered, "We will teach you!"

I would not be alone. I had more people around me there than any other place I have lived. They took good care of me.

Me. A girl from Nova Scotia moved to Louisiana, the winter home of the robins. Back in Nova Scotia, seeing a robin at the end of March is a sign that the long winter is ending. Living in Louisiana, I found out that is where the robins were coming from.

My world was turned upside down. I watched the robins in the winter. I stayed mostly inside during the summer and enjoyed the warm weather in the winter. It is the complete opposite from Nova Scotia. The dories were called peros.[40] The fiddle music had a different twist known as Cajun. The bayous were filled with live oak trees draped with Spanish moss. Gumbo, fried catfish, jambalayas, etouffees, and shrimp, boiled, fried, stewed and put in all of the above were very strange to me. The strangest of all were the crawfish piled in the middle of a table red and hot, which burned your lips for a day later. Christopher loved it and ate it all. Paul and I were not as adventurous. I was familiar with lobster; I was told the first time a Cajun saw a lobster, he thought it was the biggest crawfish he had ever seen.

Everyone owns a truck and a gun and everyone hunts. That may be an exaggeration by me, but not by much. I brought a tenth grade son and dropped him in a place so foreign, that I may as well have dropped him on the moon. This mother would not buy a toy gun for Christopher to play with when he was little. If he wanted to make a gun from a stick, that was fine with me, but I was not going to let him pretend to use a weapon.

Now there was a need to teach him about guns, for no other reason than to keep him safe. Joey said he would and he began to prepare Christopher for his first hunt. When Christopher placed the rifle on his shoulder, they all hit the deck. That is when Joey realized the lesson had to begin with 'What is a gun'?

Christopher took it upon himself to enjoy Louisiana. Today he says it was the best education he could ever have had. The seniors in high school had a tradition. Just before graduation, they would go 'mudding'. It began at sunup, everyone had four wheelers and they would hit the wilderness of the bayous. The whole idea was to see how much swamp water and mud you could drive through before school started that morning. When Christopher arrived back home, he looked like a mud monster. Yellow brown mud from head to toe. I have a picture to prove it.

Traditions

I must admit I preferred the tradition that Jennifer had as a senior in Pittsburgh. There they decorated cars and the seniors would drive to elementary school parking lots. Here the children would come out and see all the cars decorated. This encouraged the elementary students to remain in school until graduation.

Back to Louisiana and Mardi Gras. The big day was Fat Tuesday, just before the fasting of the Catholic season of Lent. Schools are out for several days for everyone to attend such things as a Rooster run, which means chasing a chicken until you catch it and put it in the gumbo for the celebration later on that evening. There are parades everywhere. As the parade passes by, you attempt to catch as many beads as you can, while they are thrown your way.

My mother attended one of these parades. We found out quickly they like to throw beads and trinkets to older people. We all stood beside Mom because her neck was filled with colourful beads. We caught her leftovers. This is Mardi Gras through my eyes. It can be a rather complicated holiday. For that reason, I will allow you to research it for further details.

Oh, yes, I must not forget 'deep fried turkey'. I have never seen a deep fried turkey, nor did I ever imagine even wanting to fry a turkey. That is how it is done in Louisiana; I must admit it tasted pretty good.

Story telling is famous in Louisiana. Stories that are handed down from generation to generation. I have one of my own to tell.

I was working on the ranch one day. I was invited to join the cowboys, hired hands and a few guests that were present for a cook out lunch. A Cajun was sitting beside me as we enjoyed our grilled steak. My boss introduced me, telling him I was from Nova Scotia.

The only reason there are Cajuns in Louisiana is that in the 1600s the English kicked out the French Acadians in Nova Scotia. They were kicked out because they would not pledge allegiance to the English during a war between France and England. Guess where they sent them. Louisiana, and not because they wanted to go. They were forced. Many generations later, the descendents of the Acadians became known as Cajuns.

Back to my story.

The Cajun asked me if I could speak French, for there are both French and English in Nova Scotia. My answer was, "No, I do not speak French. I am English. I am afraid I am one of the ones who sent you here."

My boss dropped his fork.

Mr. Cajun said, "Well, I must admit I have never sat at the same table with an enemy before."

I then apologized for my ancestors and told him I was glad to be having lunch with him. My boss never let

Traditions

me forget that day. He thought there might be a war about to start again between the English and the French.

The following is a Louisiana story that I found.

"Boudreaux live across de bayou from Clarence who he don like at all. Dey all de time yell across de bayou at each other. Boudreaux would yell to Clarence, "If I had a way to cross de bayou, I'd come over dere an beat you up good, yeah!"

Dis went on for years. Finally de state done built a bridge across dat bayou right by dere houses and Boudreaux's wife Marie say, "Now is you chance, Boudreaux. Why don't you go over dere and beat up Clarence lak you say?"

Boudreaux, "OK" and start across de bridge, but he see a sign on de bridge as he stop to read it and then he go back home.

Marie say, "Why you back so soon?"

An Boudreaux say, "Mais Marie, I don change my mind about beat up Clarence. You know, Marie, dey got a sign on dat bridge what say Clarence 13ft. 6 in. You know, he don look near dat big when I yell at him from across de bayou!" "

*****

What does the Bible say about traditions? The word means a giving over, by word of mouth or in writing. There are three types of tradition mentioned in the New Testament. First, the most common use is the kind of tradition handed down by the Jewish fathers or elders, which constituted the oral law. This is the law that the Pharisees misused and traditions became out of control.

The word tradition occurs only fourteen times in the whole New Testament, not once in the Old Testament. Eight references are from Jesus himself. Not once does he insinuate they are useful or scriptural.

> "Then some Pharisees and teachers of the law came to Jesus from Jerusalem and asked, "Why do your disciples break the tradition of the elders? They don't wash their hands before they eat."[41]

Jesus replied, "And why do you break the command of God for the sake of your tradition?". . . . Nowhere does Jesus teach there is a tradition of men and of God.

> [Jesus] replied, "Isaiah was right when he prophesied about you hypocrites; as it is written; These people honor me with their lips, but their hearts are far from me. They worship me in vain; their teachings are but rules taught

> by men. You have let go of the commands of God and are holding on to the traditions of men." [42]

The people had a choice of following commands of God or their own rules. They defaulted to their own rules that they thought were biblical.

> "So then, brothers, stand firm and hold to the teaching we passed on to you whether by word of mouth or by letter."[43]

Is this a contradiction?
What teachings or traditions is he passing on to them?
Paul previously stated:

> "Don't you remember that when I was with you I used to tell you these things?"[44]

Paul wrote down for them, and us today, what he had previously taught in person.

The only revelation we have today is what the apostles wrote down. This was what the church accepted and practiced after the death of the apostles. It was that which was written, not what is spoken today.

Paul says, "Do not go beyond what is written." That is why what was taught was penned on paper, pointing to the scripture as our final authority. Every time the Pharisees, the religious, men brought up traditions as equal to the Scripture, Jesus brought them to the word. This is why He called them the traditions of men, since they did not come from God but by religious men, who no longer intended to obey the word.

Traditions, we all have them. They are all different; your traditions are not the same as mine. Traditions are wonderful, until we bring them into the worship of God. If everyone brought his or her traditions into worship, there would be chaos. God knew that, and He gave us laws about how He wants to be worshiped.

"But, God, I want to show You my traditions. I serve them up to You." I have heard this repeatedly.

God knows how much we like our traditions. He is glad it makes us happy. That does not mean He wants you to tap dance in worship because you are good at it. Read the Scriptures; He tells us how He wants to be worshiped. When, why, how, where, He tells it all. Why can we not do it His way?

Traditions

Dear God,

I want to live for You. I know I am different from the women that live in Africa or India or Ireland. Thank You for loving me for who I am.

Thank You for the traditions the Wilcoxson family have enjoyed for many years. Thank You for the memories of raising our children.

Thank You for the doors You opened, and the experiences we have while serving You. I pray the Gospel will continue to be taken to all corners of this earth.

Father, You continue to keep us safe and have given us opportunities to meet with Your children. I pray that they will be diligent in studying Your word. Let us learn what You want us to do. Forgive us from adding to or taking away from the commands You have given us.

Help us to worship You, Your way.

I pray this in Jesus' Name.

Catherine Wilcoxson

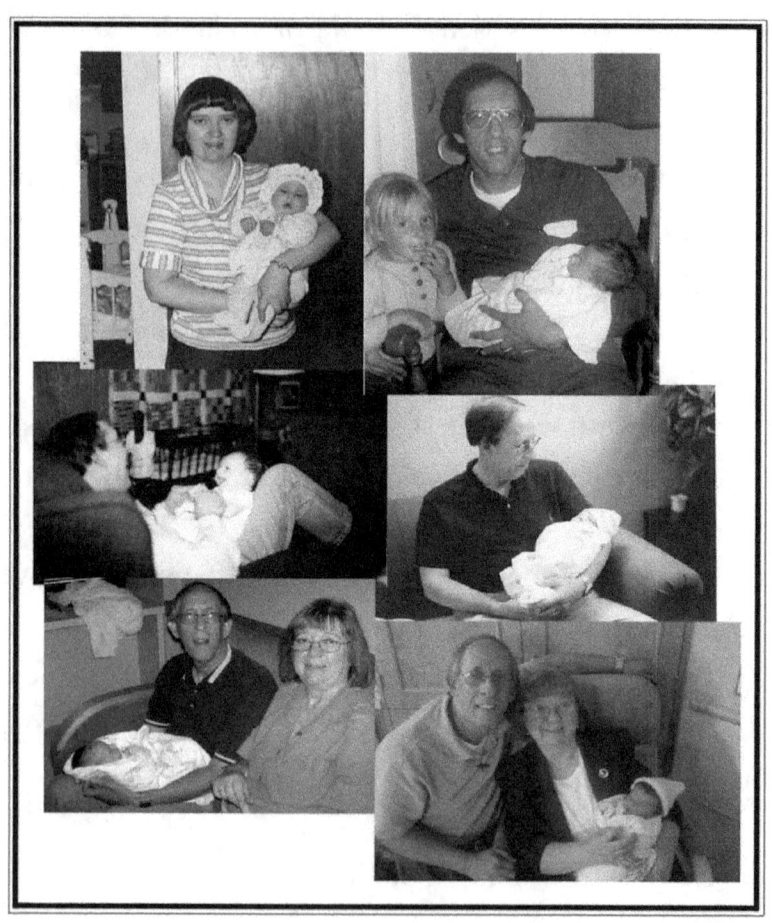

Six Babies And Counting

CHAPTER 14 NEWBORN BABIES

The Birth of Jesus Christ:

In the sixth month, God sent the angel Gabriel to Nazareth, a town in Galilee, to a virgin pledged to be married to a man named Joseph, a descendant of David. The virgin's name was Mary. The angel went to her and said, "Greetings, you who are highly favored! The Lord is with you."

Mary was greatly troubled at his words and wondered what kind of greeting this might be. But the angel said to her, "Do not be afraid Mary, you have found favor with God. You will be with child and give birth to a son, and you are to give Him the name Jesus. He will begreat and will be called the Son of the Most High. The Lord God will give him the throne of His father David, and

He will reign over the house of Jacob forever, His kingdom will never end.

"How will this be," Mary asked the angel, "since I am a virgin?"

The angel answered, "The Holy Spirit will come upon you, and the power of the Most High will overshadow you. So the holy one to be born will be called the Son of God."

"I am the Lord's servant," Mary answered. "May it be to me as you have said." Then the angel left her.

Mary was pledged to be married to Joseph, but before they came together, she was found to be with child through the Holy Spirit. Because Joseph her husband was a righteous man and did not want to expose her to public disgrace, he had in mind to divorce her quietly.

But after he had considered this, an angel of the Lord appeared to him in a dream and said, "Joseph son of David, do not be afraid to take Mary home as your wife, because what is conceived in her is from the Holy Spirit. She will give birth to a son and you are to give him the name Jesus, because he will save his people from their sins."

When Joseph woke up, he did what the angel of the Lord had commanded him and took Mary home as his wife. But he had no union with her until she gave birth to a son.

Newborn Babies

In those days, Caesar Augustus issued a decree that a census should be taken of the entire Roman world. (This was the first census that took place while Quirinius was governor of Syria.) And everyone went to his own town to register.

So Joseph also went up from the town of Nazareth in Galilee to Judea, to Bethlehem the town of David, because he belonged to the house and line of David. He went there to register with Mary, who was pledged to be married to him and was expecting a child. While they were there the time came for the baby to be born, and she gave birth to her firstborn a son. She wrapped him in cloths and placed him in a manger, because there was no room for them in the inn. Joseph named him Jesus.

And there were shepherds living out in the fields nearby, keeping watch over their flocks at night. An angel of the Lord appeared to them, and the glory of the Lord shone around them, and they were terrified. But the angel said to them, "Do not be afraid. I bring you good news of great joy that will be for all the people. Today in the town of David a Savior has been born to you; he is Christ the Lord. This will be a sign to you; You will find a baby wrapped in cloths and lying in a manger."

Suddenly a great company of the heavenly host appeared with the angel, praising God and saying, "Glory to God in the highest and on earth peace to men on whom his favor rests."

When the angels had left them and gone into heaven, the shepherds said to one another, "Let's go to Bethlehem and see this thing that has happened, which the Lord has told us about."

So they hurried off and found Mary and Joseph, and the baby, who was lying in the manger. When they had seen him, they spread the word concerning what had been told them about this child, and all who heard it were amazed at what the shepherds said to them. But Mary treasured up all these things and pondered them in her heart. The shepherds returned, glorifying and praising God for all the things they had heard and seen, which were just as they had been told.

On the eighth day, when it was time to circumcise Him, He was named Jesus, the name the angel had given Him before He had been conceived.

When the time of their purification according to the Law of Moses had been completed, Joseph and Mary took him to Jerusalem to present him to the Lord (as it is written in the Law of the Lord, "Every firstborn male is to be consecrated to the Lord") and to offer a sacrifice in keeping with what is said in the Law of the Lord: "a pair of doves or two young pigeons."

Newborn Babies

Now there was a man in Jerusalem called Simeon, who was righteous and devout. He was waiting for the consolation of Israel, and the Holy Spirit was upon him. It had been revealed to him by the Holy Spirit that he would not die before he had seen the Lord's Christ. Moved by the Spirit, he went into the temple courts. When the parents brought in the child Jesus to do for him what the custom of the Law required, Simeon took him in his arms and praised God, saying:

"Sovereign Lord, as you have promised, you now dismiss your servant in peace. For my eyes have seen your salvation, which you have prepared in the sight of all people, a light for revelation to the Gentiles and for glory to your people Israel."

The child's father and mother marveled at what was said about Him. Then Simeon blessed them and said to Mary, his mother. "This child is destined to cause the falling and rising of many in Israel, and to be a sign that will be spoken against, so that the thoughts of many hearts will be revealed. And a sword will pierce your own soul too."

There was also a prophetess, Anna, the daughter of Phanuel, of the tribe of Asher. She was very old; she had lived with her husband seven years after her marriage, and then was a widow until she was eighty-four. She never left the temple but worshiped night and day, fasting and praying. Coming up to them at that very moment, she gave thanks to God and spoke about the child to all who were looking forward to the redemption of Jerusalem.

After Jesus was born in Bethlehem in Judea, during the time of King Herod, Magi from the east came to Jerusalem and asked, "Where is the one who has been born king of the Jews? We saw his star in the east and have come to worship him."

When King Herod heard this, he was disturbed, and all Jerusalem with him. When he had called together all the people's chief priests and teachers of the law, he asked them where the Christ was to be born. "In Bethlehem in Judea," they replied, "for this is what the prophet has written. 'But you, Bethlehem, in the land of Judah, are by no means least among the rulers of Judah; for out of you will come a ruler who will be the shepherd of my people Israel.'"

Then Herod called the Magi secretly and found out from them the exact time the star had appeared. He sent them to Bethlehem and said, "Go and make a careful search for the child. As soon as you find him, report to me, so that I too may go and worship him."

After they had heard the king, they went on their way, and the star they had seen in the east went ahead of them until it stopped over the place where the child was. When they saw the star, they were overjoyed. On coming to the house, they saw the child with his mother Mary, and they bowed down and worshiped him. Then they opened their treasures and presented him with gifts of gold and of incense and of myrrh. And having been warned in a dream not to go back to Herod, they returned to their country by another route.

When they had gone, an angel of the Lord appeared to Joseph in a dream. "Get up," he said, "take the child and his mother and escape to Egypt. Stay there until I tell you, for Herod is going to search for the child to kill him."

Therefore, he got up, took the child and his mother during the night and left for Egypt, where he stayed until the death of Herod. And so was fulfilled what the Lord had said through the prophet: "Out of Egypt I called my son."

When Herod realized that he had been outwitted by the Magi, he was furious, and he gave orders to kill all the boys in Bethlehem and its vicinity who were two years old and under, in accordance with the time he had learned from the Magi. Then what was said through the prophet Jeremiah was fulfilled:

A voice is heard in Ramah, weeping and great mourning, Rachel weeping for her children and refusing to be comforted because they are no more." [45]

*****

Well, have you ever heard such a story? It would make a great movie, would it not?

Can you imagine what Mary thought? Well, first, it was bad enough that she had to spend the night in the barn, (even though it was warm). Then she gave birth to her baby beside the cattle. She did the best she could; Joseph helped her wrap the baby in cloth and laid him in the feeding trough. (I used a drawer from a hotel dresser once to make a bed for Jennifer when she was a baby. However, I do not think it counts.) Mary was doing her best. Then here comes the shepherds ringing her doorbell wanting to see the baby. Shepherds smell. If you lie down with a pig, you are going to smell like a pig. Shepherds slept with sheep, they smelled like sheep. These were strangers; strangers wanted to come see her baby. It is amazing Joseph let them through the doorway. That is until he heard their story. Joseph has been there; he already knew about angels. He let them in. Joseph stood back and watched in awe. He knew it was his job to keep this baby safe and he did it well.

Seeing a newborn baby gets you every time. Especially, a mother will never forget the first time she actually sees her baby, the baby that has been a part of her for nine months. She does not have to share this with anyone. The baby depended solely on her to survive.

Mary was no different. How happy she was to see this baby and to care for him.

Newborn Babies

I, being the mother of two, remember well the magic moment that makes time stand still. To hold Jennifer and then Christopher the first few moments of their life was special indeed.

I am a very special mother, because I got to experience that magic feeling of holding Jennifer for the first time, twice. Once in May of 1978 and again in August 2004. The feeling of awe.

"You don't believe me, do you?" It did happen.

Jennifer went into labor in August 2004 with my second grandson Ethan, Paul and I were babysitting Logan. Jennifer, having a Doula to take care of her throughout the whole process, asked if I would take care of Logan and come to the hospital the next morning. Paul and I agreed.

The next morning Paul and I arrived at the hospital to see our brand new grandson Ethan. When I entered the room, Jennifer handed me the baby. When I looked down, it was as if lightening hit me. I actually gasped, and then over and over all I could say was, "Oh, Jennifer. Oh, Jennifer. Oh, Jennifer!"

Jennifer was actually alarmed at my reaction. "Is there something wrong?" she asked.

With tears in my eyes, I still said, "Oh Jennifer, I just went back in time. This baby looks exactly the same as when I gave birth to you."

Jennifer replied, "What? You scared me, Mom."

"You don't understand," I replied. "This baby is exactly the same as the baby I gave birth to. Only she is a he."

Everyone laughed. However, they still did not understand what just happened to me. That same evening I brought Jennifer's baby picture that was taken when she was born, for everyone to see. The resemblance of her and Ethan was uncanny. When the doctor and nurses saw the picture, they asked, "How did you get that picture so quickly?"

I answered, "It is not baby Ethan; it is baby Jennifer."

The doctor and nurses were amazed. And so was I.

*****

It was in the fall of 1978. Paul and I were invited to go to a 'Marriage Encounter'. We left Jennifer for the first time with Ron and Rita Pauls. Their daughters were excited to have a baby to play with.

'Marriage Encounter' is a weekend where couples learn to communicate and get to know each other by writing letters back and forth to each other. The subject of one letter was, "What are the three times that you felt closest to your mate?"

Paul wrote:

1. The time we were first engaged to be married.
2. The birth of Jennifer.
3. Sharing my fears I have in this life.

This is what he wrote to me about number two, the birth of Jennifer.

"Dear Cathy;

The next occasion of closeness was as you were giving birth to Jennifer. I knew I was supposed to be strong and comfort you, but inside I felt so inadequate. I felt like someone who saw another drowning and was helpless to assist. But somehow God gave me strength and I was happy to be there with you. I was so grateful to be able to share this most intimate relationship with you. The giving of life to our own daughter thrilled me beyond explanation. Now, knowing that we brought a child into the world and it was because of our love makes me proud to be your husband and that we share this most wonderful privilege together.

To be able to mould a little one to know God is truly remarkable."

Another letter subject was "The reason for wanting to go on living." The second part of Paul's letter reads:

"I want to go on living because of our little Jennifer. I want to thank you from the bottom of my heart for your carrying her inside you Cathy, and for your nurturing her until she was prepared to enter this world. I owe you so much for the gift of our lovely daughter and now that we have her, it gives me another reason for wanting to go on living. She is such a fragile little thing, whose every need has to be met at this time. I realize that her personality is hers and hers alone, yet her life how it turns out will be partially determined by how I teach her. Knowing this and knowing that she has so many needs, I want to go on living for her. I had a great part in bringing her into the world, so I have a great responsibility to train her to know and love God and to get along in a cruel world that so often is so unloving and so unkind. I want to mold her little life to know and love God as I know and love Him. But at the same time, I want her faith to be her own, not simply a reflection of mine. Still, I want to be around, so that I can provide her with the best example of what a Christian father and husband should be. Perhaps in this way, she will be able to choose a mate of her own when she is old enough to consider starting a home of her own. I know that Jennifer needs a father to give her a true picture of who a man is and what his relationship in the human family is. In order to have a complete and rounded personality, she must have the influence of a loving caring Christian father.

I want to go on living because I want to see Jennifer grow, mature, and blossom into the beautiful rose of womanhood and to see her place her hand in the Lords and walk together with Him as long as she lives. I want to see the results of the long hours, days, months and years of training produce a lovely Christian young lady. To be able to see this and know that everything has paid off will be to me as it was to Simeon when he saw the baby Jesus and said, "Now let your servant die in peace, for my own eyes have seen Thy Salvation." I truly believe that to know this had paid off would be a life well spent and truly satisfying.

I am finding that this writing is causing me to really think. I have poured my heart out to you about why I want to go on living."

One other letter I want to share with you that Paul wrote. "What are my feelings when I see our children respond to you?"

"Dear Sweetie,

Well, I cannot say "children". I have to say "child". I find this hard I guess.

When I think of Jennifer's responding to you, I feel proud. I am pleased to think of this because Jennifer is an extension of my love to

Newborn Babies

you. She is part of both of us, yet a separate being within herself. All this is complicated and hard to grasp.

I feel humbled to know that we have both played a part in bringing a human being into the world, which is a miracle in itself. And to have the privilege of moulding a little life and seeing her respond to you or to me simply astounds me. I can only give glory and praise to God who made it all possible.

To see her respond in the way that she is trained to go gives a feeling of satisfaction in a job well done. Of course, we'll never know for certain how she'll turn out till she is grown. But if we train her to know the Lord and to love Him, I believe she will turn out all right.

I don't know whether my letter so far is answering the question fully. All I can think of is how Jennifer relates to you and how well she seems to respond to teaching and the like. I really feel great to see her get along so well with you most of the time. I realize the need to set a good example before her, and to always try to keep the same relationship with her as we have now. Just maybe that will make the difference between a good relationship and a great one.

Love you,

Paul"

Now you know why I thank God for sending me this man from Tennessee.

*****

Have you ever had a second chance? You might call it a new birth.

You may have messed it up the first time. If you were offered a second chance, would you not jump at it?

Or, do you ever wish you could live some of those years over again? Maybe you would do parts of it just a little differently. We look back and we know we cannot. There may be bits of time you wish you could forget. You were not proud of it at the time, and you are not proud of it today.

What if I told you that it is okay? Jesus knows what has happened in your past. He knows how difficult it is for you. What if Jesus said you could start all over? What if He would give you a clean slate? The mistakes in your past will be taken away. Gone.

Newborn Babies

Jesus offers you a new birth. He offered it to me and He offers it to you.

"Now there was a man of the Pharisees named Nicodemus, a member of the Jewish ruling council. He came to Jesus at night and said, "Rabbi, we know you are a teacher who has come from God. For no one could perform the miraculous signs you are doing if God were not with him."[46]

In reply, Jesus declared:

"I tell you the truth, no one can see the kingdom of God unless he is born again."

"How can a man be born when he is old?" Nicodemus asked. "Surely he cannot enter a second time into his mother's womb to be born!"

Jesus answered, "I tell you the truth, no one can enter the kingdom of God unless he is born of water and the Spirit.

Flesh gives birth to flesh, but the Spirit gives birth to spirit. You should not be surprised at my saying, 'You must be born again.' The wind blows wherever it pleases. You hear its sound, but you cannot tell where it comes from or where it is going. So it is with everyone born of the Spirit."

"How can this be?" Nicodemus asked.

"You are Israel's teacher," said Jesus, "and do you not understand these things? I tell you the truth, we speak of what we know, and we testify to what we have seen, but still you people do not accept our testimony. I have spoken to you of earthly things and you do not believe; how then will you believe if I speak of heavenly things? No one has ever gone into heaven except the one who came from heaven--the Son of Man. Just as Moses lifted up the snake in the desert, so the Son of Man must be lifted up, that everyone who believes in him may have eternal life.

"For God so loved the world that he gave his one and only Son, that whoever believes in him shall not perish but have eternal life. For God did not send his Son into the world to condemn the world, but to save the world through him. Whoever believes in him is not condemned, but whoever does not believe stands condemned already because he has not believed in the name of God's one and only Son. This is the verdict: Light has come into the world, but men loved darkness instead of light because their deeds were evil. Everyone who does evil hates the light, and will not come into the light for fear that his deeds will be exposed. But whoever lives by the truth comes into the light, so that it may be seen plainly that what he has done has been done through God." [47]

Newborn Babies

Dear God,

Thank You. How can I thank You more? I wish I had the words to tell You how much I thank You for Jesus.

Thank You for Mary. And for Joseph. They both took great care to see that Jesus grew up from the baby they placed in the manger that night so long ago.

Thank You for the shepherds. Shepherds were not well liked; they were looked down upon. Yet You chose them to hear the good news first.

Help me not to look down upon anyone. Help me show them the love You have for us all.

Thank You for Jennifer and Christopher; they were beautiful babies. They grew up to be wonderful adults. Protect them from the evil of this world.

Thank You for the gift, the man from Tennessee. For I love him dearly.

In Jesus Name I pray.
Catherine Wilcoxson

Cows At Smokey Cove

CHAPTER 15 KNEE-KNOCKING FEAR

King Belshazzar gave a great banquet for a thousand of his nobles and drank wine with them.

"While Belshazzar was drinking his wine, he gave orders to bring in the gold and silver goblets that Nebuchadnezzar his father had taken from the temple in Jerusalem, so that the king and his nobles, his wives and his concubines might drink from them.

Therefore, they brought in the gold goblets that had been taken from the temple of God in Jerusalem, and the king and his nobles, his wives and his concubines drank from them.

As they drank the wine, they praised the gods of gold and silver, of bronze, wood, and stone.

Suddenly the fingers of a human hand appeared and wrote on the plaster of the wall, near the lampstand in the royal palace. The king watched the hand as it wrote.

His face turned pale and he was so frightened that his knees knocked together and his legs gave way.

The king called out for the enchanters, astrologers and diviners to be brought, and said to these wise men of Babylon, "Whoever reads this writing and tells me what it means will be clothed in purple and have a gold chain placed around his neck, and he will be made the third highest ruler in the kingdom."

Then all the king's wise men came in, but they could not read the writing or tell the king what it meant.

So King Belshazzar became even more terrified and his face grew more pale. His nobles were baffled.

The queen, hearing the voices of the king and his nobles, came into the banquet hall. "O king, live forever!" she said. "Do not be alarmed! Do not look so pale!"

There is a man in your kingdom who has the spirit of the holy gods in him. In the time of your father, he was found to have insight, intelligence, and wisdom like that of the gods. King Nebuchadnezzar your father--your father the king, I say--appointed him chief of the magicians, enchanters, astrologers and diviners.

Knee-Knocking Fear

This man Daniel, whom the king called Belteshazzar, was found to have a keen mind and knowledge and understanding, and the ability to interpret dreams, explain riddles and solve difficult problems. Call for Daniel, and he will tell you what the writing means."

King Belshazzar had every right to have knee-knocking fear. He messed with the true God. Using the gold goblets from the Temple of God in Jerusalem was not a good idea. Especially to honor the gods of gold, silver, bronze, iron, wood, and stone.

The God of Creation was not pleased. And look out when this happens. Daniel came and told the bad news to the king.

O Belshazzar you have not humbled yourself, though you knew better. Instead, you have set yourself up against the Lord of heaven. Misusing the goblets from his temple, therefore he sent the hand that wrote the inscription, Mene, Mene, Tekel, Parsin.

This is what these words mean:

Mene: God has numbered the days of your reign and brought it to an end.

Tekel: You have been weighed on the scales and found wanting.

Peres: Your kingdom is divided and given to the Medes and Persians.

That very night, Belshazzar, king of the Babylonians was slain." [48]

*****

Fear. That is a scary word. Fear. Knee knocking fear. When you say the word fear, everyone can relate to it.

Everyone is afraid of something. Millions of dollars are paid out yearly for people to get help with their fears. Fears of many kinds. Such as fear of spiders Arachnophobia, fear of heights Batophobia, fear of small spaces Claustrophobia, large areas Agoraphobia. Fear of elevators, escalators, Ferris wheels and the ThunderBolt Roller Coaster.

We all have a list of fears. Some lists are longer for some than others. Fears can be large or small. They can affect how you live. There are people who have a fear of leaving their house. They cannot go out the front door.

I would say my list of fears is a moderate one. My fears do not drastically change my ability to live my life. When I put myself in the pathway of my fears, my heart races, and, of course, I want to retreat. We all want to run from our fears. That is not always good. Every time you run from your fears, that fear usually grows and gets stronger and makes it even harder to face the next time.

Knee-Knocking Fear

I believe it is a learning process and to face fears head on gives you a feeling of freedom and accomplishment.

My fear of the ThunderBolt and the Racers, the two roller coasters at Kennywood Amusement Park in Pittsburgh, Pennsylvania was definitely a real one for me. No way was I going to put myself on a ride that would scare me to death. However, of course, I was talked into it. The Racers was a wooden roller coaster with two tracks and two different cars racing beside each other. The race was on to see which car would reach the bottom first. I really didn't care.

Friends said, "But you need to go on one once – just so you could tell your grandchildren you did it!"

Why I fell for such reasoning is beyond me; I did not even have grandchildren at the time. However, I did fall for it. Here I was belted into this ride with my kids and my good friend, Patti, and her daughter, Sarah.

I can remember telling myself repeatedly, "I can do anything for three minutes. I can do anything for three minutes." I closed my eyes tightly and never saw a thing around me. I have no idea whether we won or not. All I wanted to do was get off that thing. Never again. However, I must admit, I was glad I faced that fear. If for some reason I had to do it again, I know I could.

*****

Being a city girl and finding myself working on a ranch in Louisiana was completely out of my comfort zone. Nevertheless, I found it fascinating. Walking along the lane, I would talk to the cows as they grazed just on the other side of the fence. They would look up, wondering what I was trying to tell them. I referred to them as "happy cows," for to me they looked happy enough. They had food as far as the eye could see. The cows were beautiful, if you could call cows beautiful.

One day I was alone at the ranch working in the house. My boss asked me to watch over a cow that was about to give birth to her calf. When the blessed event began, I was to phone for help.

Every half-hour I would go and look. I would climb up the gate to the fence to take a good look. Did you notice something here? I would not go on the other side of the fence. No way did I want to be on the other side of the fence when the cows were walking around. I was told they would not hurt me. That did not matter, for anything that big put fear into me. I did my duty; I could tell the blessed event was happening, and I made the phone call.

Another day I was alon working in the house. I looked out the window, and five of the biggest, most beautiful light-brown cows you ever saw were walking down the laneway. They were not behind the fence; they had escaped. Now, what in the world was I going to do? I just could not ignore it. That was not an option. All I could see were $$$ signs walking towards the house, and soon would be towards the road. Those cows were worth a great deal more than $25,000 each.

Fear came up in my throat. My heart was beating fast, and I had sweat on my hands because I knew I had to do something. However, I couldn't go out there and meet those cows head on. "They will not listen to me; they will just run me over." My fear was telling me I could not. However, my brain was telling me, "You had better do something about the cows."

"Okay, I will. I will." The broom. Why I thought of a broom, I do not know. I believe there was an angel watching over me. An angel that did not know anything about cows either.

I grabbed the broom and ran out waving it and yelling, "Go back, you cows. Go back!"

To my amazement, the cows stopped in their tracks. They just stared at me. "So far so good," I thought. I started waving the broom again and yelling, "Go back, you cows. Go back," as I walked forward.

Those cows have never seen such a crazy lady waving a broom and yelling to the top of her lungs before. They turned around and ran back through the open gate.

I ran up, closed the gate, and said, "Now, you cows stay there."

Then I heard clapping, whistling, and laughing. I turned around and there stood Carl and Huey, the real cowboys that worked the ranch.

"How long have you guys been here?" I asked.

Their answer, "We saw you coming with the broom. We stayed out of your way. Best entertainment we have had all day," said Carl.

Those cowboys liked me. That is to say a lot, for they did not like city folks. That was not the only time I entertained them.

I heard them comment to my boss, "When Catherine has a problem; she thinks it through and takes action. May not be the way we do it, but the job gets done."

I took that as a very nice compliment, for this city girl loved being on the ranch.

The ranch was a beautiful place. My mother was visiting from Nova Scotia for the winter. On a nice day in early spring, I took her for a ride on a "mule," a very small utility vehicle. We spent eight hours riding around the ranch. My mother loved it, and I have the greatest memory a daughter could ever have spending a great day with my mother.

*****

Knee-Knocking Fear

Midlife crisis. What does it mean? You may be halfway through your life and you are not sure you like it.

I was going through a midlife crisis. I was about to turn fifty years old. I was tired. Actually, I was tired of working with people. At least I thought I was. That is one thing about a midlife crisis, you do not think very clearly.

God must look down and just shake His head, "Look what I have done for you, and you still aren't happy."

"Well, God, I am tired of working with people. They are difficult, you know. You never know what they are going to do. And after all, the things I do for them."

People who go through midlife crises do irrational things. Some get a new husband. "No, that would not do. I like my old one." Or they buy a sports car. "No, I don't have the money. What can I do? I want it to be good, God. I want it to stand out. Something that is wild but not too wild. Dangerous, but not too dangerous. Scary, but fun scary. Do you have anything in mind, God?"

And God did! Horses!

No, I did not get a new husband, and I could not afford a sports car, so I did horses.

The ranch was full of horses. I went to my boss and asked him if Jennifer and I could come once a week and do horses. Jennifer knew all about horses, so I would not be doing horses by myself.

My boss laughed. The cowboys laughed. "Sure, you can do horses." Whatever that meant, they knew it would last a couple weeks, and that would be it.

I forgot to mention one thing. I am scared to death of horses. I love horses; they are beautiful animals. I love horses, just like the cows on the other side of the fence. My fear of horses outweighs my fear of cows.

This was my midlife and I wanted to do something completely different. Step out of the box or out of your comfort zone, as they say it.

I announced to Paul that Jennifer and I were going to do horses every Tuesday night. In addition, he was going to babysit his grandson Logan. I think he was surprised, not because he would be babysitting, but that I was going to do horses.

The first Tuesday came. That was all I could think about all day. I almost backed out three times. However, Jennifer would not let me do that. It was a warm spring evening. We parked beside the Tack Room. We put oats in a bucket, and Jennifer carried it towards the gate that opened into a large field. She opened the gate and we entered the field. The reason we got that far was that I could not see any horses. However, my heart was racing, for I was on the other side of the fence.

Jennifer said, "Watch this." She started banging on the bucket and calling, "Here, horsey. Here horsey." Now, on the other side of the field, I saw them. My heart jumped into my throat, for several horses heard Jennifer's call, and they were coming our way. Not just coming, they were galloping, trying to race each other to get to us.

All I can remember was screaming, turning and running as fast as I could towards the gate. I left Jennifer, my daughter, and ran for my life. I just got on the other side of the fence when three horses arrived there, and they were not walking! I thought I was going to pass out. When I thought of poor Jennifer, I said, "She is probably dead." I screamed, "Jennifer!" I could not see her. I had left her sort of around the bend.

She appeared, laughing her head off, with three or four horses wanting the oats from her bucket. "Did you see that? Wasn't that the greatest thing you ever saw? Are you okay? I saw several horses going your way?"

"All right? Am I all right? I thought you were dead and I barely survived."

Her laughter was contagious; I started laughing too.

The second Tuesday came. I was panicking all day. However, I fought through and found myself once more at the Tack Room putting oats in a bucket.

I told Jennifer there was no way I was going inside that field this week.

She said, "Okay, Mom. This is what we will do. We will bring one of the horses out to the paddock and give him a bath and rubdown. Let's go."

"Sure, let's go," I thought. We got to the same gate. She banged on the bucket, and, magically after a few moments, we saw horses thundering towards us. This time I took in how beautiful it really was. However, that was because I was on the other side of the fence.

Jennifer held up a bridle. "I am going in get a horse. Then we will bring him out. Now I need your help."

All of a sudden, my heart was in my throat again.

"What?"

"You can do this, Mom"

"Do What?"

"When I am ready you need to open the gate. But you have to make sure the other horses do not come out too."

"How am I going to do that?"

"Quickly," Jennifer said. Looking at me, she just laughed. "You can do it!"

I laughed, "Okay. Let's do it."

I do not know how I did it, but I did. She came out leading a horse, and I quickly closed the gate in front of several other horses that wanted out too.

Knee-Knocking Fear

She led the horse and tied him. Then she passed the water hose to me and turned it on. We were going to give the horse a cool shower. The horse loved it. That was the first time I was this close to a horse. My fear was still there, for the pictures Jennifer took showed that I was two or three yards away while spraying water on his back. I thought I was close.

The third Tuesday we were back. This time my gatekeeping did not go as well. I allowed two other horses to come through the gate before I could close it.

Now here was Jennifer leading a horse, and two more were out. I was panicking, and Jennifer said it was okay. She tied her horse to the fence and recaptured the other two. My gatekeeping was a little better, for we got them back into the field without allowing any more out.

After two more weeks of doing horses went by, Jennifer decided it was time for me to lead the horse back to the field, as soon as we cleaned and brushed him.

"Mom, you can do this," was always what she said. With my heart beating like a drum, I took the bridle and we began to walk, just the horse and me. Jennifer was taking pictures.

I remember exactly what was going on in my mind to this day. "Catherine, you can do this. Look straight ahead. You've got the horse's head; the rest will just follow along."

I will always remember that night. My boss and the cowboys were impressed. Six weeks straight I would come and "play" with horses, as they called it. They asked the dreaded question, "When are you going to ride?"

I answered, "I believe Jennifer and I need a lesson on saddles and bridles, and which saddles go with which horses."

"Great, we will be there Tuesday night."

Now I was in trouble. The following Tuesday was here, and all I could say throughout the day was, "I am in big trouble." For I knew if two cowboys and the owner of this ranch were going to show up and give us a lesson on saddling horses, that only meant one thing.

If they were going to put saddles on horses, that meant someone was going to ride the horse. There was no way around it.

That is actually what happened. Jennifer was thrilled. My boss took us horseback riding. It was like being out in Africa, open country as far as the eye could see. The deer, the sunset, and the darkness falling around us would have been a wonderful sight, if my ankles did not ache with pain. Added to that was the fear that the horse would not go any faster than a walk. I could hardly get him to do that. The reigns did not work as easily as a gas pedal in a car. When we got back, it was dark. All I could think

Knee-Knocking Fear

of was, "How am I going to get off this horse?" It looked more like falling off when I reached the ground.

I was not ready to quit yet! During the next week, I asked the cowboys why my ankles hurt so badly. They informed me that the stirrups needed adjusting.

The next Tuesday Jennifer was ready to ride again. There would be no more of the cleaning of horses. Carl showed us how to adjust my stirrup and he said, "Okay, on the horse."

I complained that it was so high that I could not put my foot up that high and then swing myself up.

"Okay, Catherine, I will be right back." Carl left, and I thought this is the reason he does not like city slickers.

To my surprise, he reappeared with a step ladder. We all laughed. However, when he placed it by the horse, I quickly climbed up on it and placed myself in the saddle.

I enjoyed my ride much more that day. We did horses for more than a year. One other time, Jennifer and I arrived to find our horses in another field, and we couldn't even see them. We knocked on Carl's door and he was not very happy; he had just finished his working day and just wanted to watch TV. "All you have to do is call them."Seeing our blank faces he said, "You don't know how to do that, do you? Okay, let's go." Carl came out in his house slippers and let out this piercing cry,

"HORSEEEEEEE." He only had to do it twice when we heard the thundering sound of horse hooves. The whole herd was coming. Jennifer and I were very impressed. Carl went back to his TV. Jennifer learned to do the 'HORSEEEEEE'; I never could get the hang of it.

After the time we disturbed Carl, my boss decided if we wanted to do horses, we should do them during the cowboy's working hours. Carl was happy and we didn't mind at all. One afternoon we came, and, again, our horses were in yet another field. This time there were fences between them and us. "How are we going to go ride them?" I asked Jennifer.

"Well, we can't bring the horses here to saddle them; let's take the saddles to them." We loaded up our trunk of the car with saddles and drove to the field where the horses were. Jennifer caught Roper and Stormy, placed bridles on them and tied them to the fence. We then put saddles on and had a very pleasant afternoon of horse riding.

We had family outings where we would saddle horses for everyone in the family. Thanksgiving Christopher, Kayla, and her sister, Megan, visited from niversity. There were seven of us horseback riding for miles and miles.

Knee-Knocking Fear

My fear never did go away completely. I did learn to ride a horse. I was only allowed to ride ONE horse. His name was Roper. He was old and did not have enough get up and go to hurt anyone. I loved that horse.

However, like all good things, horse riding ended. Jennifer was expecting Ethan. There would be no more horse riding. We did go to visit, but preachers come and preachers go caught up with us once more. We moved to California.

Remember, we all have fear. It is how we live with our fear that counts.

Dear God,

Thank You for allowing me to experience times on the ranch. These are years of fond memories and a good time in my life.

Thank You for the five senses that You have given me. To see, to hear, to smell, to feel, to taste. I experienced them all on the ranch.

To feel is one of the senses that can give us problems. I believe this is where fear lives. Help us to keep this feeling of fear in control.

Forgive us of our sin. This is surely a lack of self-control.

Help me live for You.

In Jesus' name,

Catherine Wilcoxson

Smokey Cove

CHAPTER 16 - IT'S A WONDERFUL LIFE

Let me paint a picture.

I am sitting on an outdoor wooden glider bench, the kind that rocks back and forth smoothly and with ease. The stress that surrounds my life, I have placed on a shelf somewhere in the back of my mind. Things like the never-ending job of cleaning the kitchen, grocery lists, piles of laundry and what to cook for dinner.

A gentle breeze passes by and I gently push my hair back and feel the coolness upon my face. The breeze continues and rattles the leaves in the Eucalyptus trees. Their branches, swaying in the wind, allow the smell like scented candles to lightly fill the air.

I glide back and forth on the raised veranda watching the panoramic view of a landscaped picture before me. The cabin is on the rise of the land, not really a hill, for there are not any hills in South Western Louisiana. However, it is high enough to see down upon the land as it slightly falls in front of me. A field runs to the bottom of the incline where a small lake, or maybe you could call it a very large pond, is placed. At the edge of the lake stand a few old trees that have battle scars of facing more than one hurricane. A small windmill faces into the wind, causing the letter "R" to spin to whichever direction the wind will take it.

This small lake is half-filled with water plants. You would think a frog could cross from shore to shore without even touching the water. White cranes with their long stick legs walk among the plants. With a flash, their heads drop to the water and bring up a fish that is swallowed in one gulp. The brown cranes are also there. However, it takes a good eye to see them, for they disappear into their surroundings.

On the other side of the lake, the land rises again. Here there is a small grove of the mighty pine trees. The foot-long pinecones lay at the trunks, waiting for my grandchildren to collect them.

Up over the rise lies more pasture which stretches out as far as the horizon and beyond towards where the sky meets the earth. The white clouds, which have just come from the Gulf of Mexico, race across the sky. You may see buzzards gather. You are not sure if they are just having a meeting in the sky, or they have found a meal to feast upon.

My eyes are drawn to the right. I have company. A small herd of cows is slowly making their way across the land bridge. Some stop and wade in the shallow water to drink or just to cool down. The leader then bellows, signaling it is time to move on. They all walk along the cow path, which is only six inches wide. It amazes me for such large animals to follow in single order. It looks like they are walking a tightrope, which you may have seen in a circus. They are coming closer to me; twenty-five or maybe thirty cows are coming right up to the cabin. They haven't noticed me as yet, for they don't encounter many people in the middle of this ranch.

All of a sudden all heads are raised. I have been spotted. The babysitter cow (didn't know cows had babysitters did you?) sent out a warning, and like magic, she has several young calves gathering around her. After seeing I was not a threat, the young calves went back to playing. Soon they all lay down for a nap.

Before long, the leader bellows again to move on. The calves wake up and scatter in all directions. This time they are looking for their own mother. It is lunchtime for them.

Just left of the land bridge is a two-tiered water dock. The upper deck is covered by a green roof. Under this green roof, you will find an outdoor kitchen set up. On the lower deck, several glider chairs and benches are available to those who like to relax in the sun. If my grandsons were here, they would be throwing rocks into the water.

This panoramic view in front of me is in a state of perpetual motion. The view changes by the minute, by the hour, and by the season, all depending upon the direction of the wind and weather. In the spring, the pastureland is full of white blossoms from the wild blackberry bushes that spread over the fields like a spider's web. Many blackberry picking parties have followed. In the winter, I have seen this whole picture covered with white frost, Louisiana's snow.

I am sitting here rocking back and forth. Quite contented indeed for this is my most favorite place in Louisiana. I come to Smokey Cove wounded and beaten down by the struggles of life. I leave regenerated and ready for the next open door God puts in front of me.

Paul and I have spent several Christmas holidays at Smokey Cove. We have made sweet, sweet memories with our dear grandsons Logan, Ethan and Connor. They love to come to Smokey Cove. We have what we call adventures. We walk for miles. Last year even two-year-old Connor walked along the cow path for a mile and a half. Mind you, it took us four hours, with snack breaks where we lie on the ground and look up at the blue sky. We see clouds in the shape of ducks and horses and we tell stories of where they may be going. Big brothers Logan and Ethan ride their bikes and can ride as far ahead as they like. Connor and I catch up when his brothers take a break of their own and are sitting on the grass waiting for us.

The adventure that we always take is walking down to the lake, crossing the land bridge to the other side. We walk through the grove of pine trees, praying a large pinecone does not fall on our heads. The boys fill up their bags with pinecones that scatter the ground. We then come to our favourite place. An old tree stump is left among the tall trees. The boys jump up on it and we take pictures. Behind them are the lake and an incline where the cabin stands. We only see these boys twice a year. These pictures reveal the growth spurts they have between adventures.

On these adventures when I know there may be cows around I take a broom. You know me; I like to be on the other side of the fence. However, there are no fences here. We have to cross a small creek; what better time to hold up my broom and part the Red Sea. Ethan was Moses; he held the broom high and made sure we crossed the stream, at least without getting wet.

Paul and I have started new traditions on Christmas morning at Smokey Cove while waiting for the Boyle family to arrive. One is breakfast gifts. I think we are too old for Santa. These are small personal gifts that we share with each other. Another tradition is, while preparing the turkey for the oven, we watch our favorite movie, "It's A Wonderful Life".

Jimmy Stewart and Donna Reed remind us how important we are and how our lives touch so many other lives. Whether or not we have a guardian angel working on our behalf to earn his wings, we do have God that loves us. God watches over us for our ultimate good.

If we had never been born, the lives of people and the events of history would be changed. Our lives affect people in ways we don't know or understand. Jimmy Stewart's character, George Bailey, didn't realize how wealthy he was because of his many friendships. Every time you hear a bell ring, it can remind you that you are not alone and you have friends all around you.

When you feel alone, and the world is pressing down upon you, remember that God is always with you.

> "God has said, "Never will I leave you; never will I forsake you." So we say with confidence, "The Lord is my helper; I will not be afraid. What can man do to me?"[49]

During times of struggle, and when it seemed the darkest, God carried us through. Paul and I have had a good life, and we thank God for those whose lives we have touched.

It's A Wonderful Life

Dear God,

Thank You for the refuge we have at Smokey Cove. A place we can shut out the world around us and feel Your presence.

A place where You recharge our batteries and give us strength to send us out again to work in Your Kingdom.

Thank You for a Wonderful Life.

In Jesus Name I pray.

Catherine

Our Home In Covington, Indiana

CHAPTER 17 - NOW WHAT?

Here I sit at my desk in my upstairs office in Covington, Indiana. This whole book has been written from this desk. I love to come into my office to write. I love my surroundings, for I feel at home here, just my computer and me. Beyond my computer, I have a wall that displays my posters and newspaper articles that tell when I became an author. My first book was *The Adventures of Captain Heman Kenney and Lady Catherine 1833-1917*. That was a very exciting time.

Sharing the wall with my author accomplishments is artwork that Jennifer did in Junior High School. It is a screen painting of pink and white tulips. It is hard for me to believe how many years have passed since she brought it home from school. Just below this cherished picture is a small corkboard. A photo of Blake sitting with very young Ethan and Logan and a photo of my mother and her sister Alice is pinned alongside a scary jack-o-lantern and a self-portrait of the artist, our grandson Ethan. They are a gift sent to me, drawings he did in 1st grade. An unusual item is an apple pincushion that has uneven stitches that form the letters "To my dear mother." I made that for my mother when I was seven. And to finish up the helter-skelter arrangement are two cards that come with delivered flowers. One reads "Happy Valentine's Day I will always be your Valentine, Love Paul." The other is "Happy Anniversary. All my love always, Paul." Oh, yes, a few ribbons hang there, blue for first, red for second and white for third. They are my prizes for entering the county fair. I always enter something each year.

Across the room is a love seat. A homemade quilt is hanging above. This quilt was given to me from a group of sweet ladies, one being our dear friend, Mama Lou, from Summertown, Tennessee. When Paul and I were first married, we were known as missionaries. When we visited the churches that supported us, one being Summertown, I was given a quilt. I love these quilts for, they are made with love and if you look closely, you will see they are not perfect. For this I love them even more, for none of us are perfect, not one. Most of the ladies are gone to be with the Lord now. They would smile to know that I now make my own quilts.

There is one window, where today it is open and the curtains are moving in the breeze. There is a huge Maple tree in full view and birds are congregating at the bird feeders. I have a wonderful view of hills and trees. Many times, I have looked out this window to see deer, wild turkey, raccoons and even unwanted visits made by a skunk or two. To the right is my favorite tree, Big Bertha. She is a sycamore that is growing down in a creek bed. Her trunk begins ten feet below in the drop off along the creek. Then she reaches up to a hundred feet or more into the sky spreading her branches where all the birds hold meetings.

Under the window are three bookshelves. Along with books, there is a collection of Fisher Price children's toys. The ones they no longer make and are collector items. My children never broke a toy. We bought several Fisher Price toys back then. Such as the yellow bus, the red barn, the Ferris wheel, the airplane, the camping set, the policemen set, the musical TV and the apple rolly polly.Every one of them is known as a choking hazard to young children today. Years ago, we were visiting a friend of Christopher's while he was at Abilene Christian University. She had Fisher Price toys on display in her den. I whispered to Christopher that I have boxes of that stuff. Turns out, they are worth something. One other toy adds to the collection. A red Tonka fire truck that has been played with by my brother, Blair, as a young boy, Greg and Ryan, my two nephews, my son, Christopher, and my grandsons, Logan and Ethan. I used it as a decoration when we honored the fire department with a dinner. Many of the older firefighters came up to me and wanted to buy it. I keep things I like around me, for they hold fond memories. Maybe it is because we move around so often. I just bring my life with me.

Besides the pictures of my children graduating high school, I have one other thing that sits here that I can see and enjoy. It is one hundred and twenty-one years old. Not worth any money, but to me, it is like holding history in my hand. It is a piece of barn board about a foot and a half long. It is taken from a barn that was on the old homestead where my mother was raised. I received it when I joined my mother for a reunion of her family in Alberta, Canada. What is unusual about this reunion is that I had never met anyone from her side of the family. I was the only one in my family who had not taken a trip west from Nova Scotia to meet the McConaghy side of the family. I did so when we lived in California. I got to see the one-room schoolhouse and the very desk my mother sat in as a child. In addition, the school house barn where they kept their horses while attending school. They were tearing down an old barn. My family wanted to give me something to remember the trip. My answer was, "I would like a piece of that barn."

My Uncle Tom, my mother's brother answered, "That is easy enough to do." And he went over to the pile of old boards and broke a piece over his knee. "Is that big enough?" he asked.

I had everyone at the reunion sign my piece of the 1890 barn. The years between 1890 and July 2005, I wonder in my mind who built it. I am sure they were a strong branch of my family tree.

Enough reminiscing. I need to get back to work. I have to write this last chapter. "Now What?" or "What Now?"

I do hope you have enjoyed me sharing my journey with you. I pray it will make you think and give you the desire to pick up that dusty Bible on your bookshelf. To open it and find the great mystery and secrets that lie within.

> "In reading this, then, you will be able to understand my insight into the mystery of Christ, which was not made known to men in other generations as it has now been revealed by the Spirit to God's holy apostles and prophets. This mystery is that through the gospel the Gentiles are heirs together with Israel, members together of one body, and sharers together in the promise in Christ Jesus." [50]

The year 2011 has been a year of struggle for both Paul and me. Paul had back surgery, which was successful. His pain is gone. We thank God.

My heart has been out of rhythm for five months. The Ablation procedure I was waiting for had been moved up three times, for they were afraid I would have a stroke.

I spent most of my time sitting in a chair, actually three chairs. One was here at my computer writing this book, one was sitting at my dining room table quilting and the other was in my living room watching out the window as winter passed me by.

That procedure was done five weeks ago today. I wasn't going to include this experience in this book, but because it was such an unusual one, I have changed my mind.

Just a few days before I was scheduled to go to the hospital, I received a phone call from my son Christopher. He informed me he was taking a special leave from work. He was allowed a week to take care of ailing parents. He was bringing Lily and they were going to help Paul take care of me after I returned home from the hospital.

I arrived at the hospital at 10:45 a.m. the day of the procedure. I was taken into pre-op where I had my blood tested and an IV was attempted. I was on Coumadin, a blood thinner. The INR rate for the operation was to be in the range of two and three. For weeks, I had been monitored to have a perfect reading.

Pre-op was not going well. I have very small veins; it took over an hour and nine tries to finally get an IV going. Then I heard someone say, "We have a lady with an INR of 3.8 Coumadin reading."

I remember thinking, "Oh my, that it is high." Turns out it was ME. Way to high to do surgery. There was a real threat of bleeding.

The doctor decided to wait it out. Every hour my blood was tested. Slowly my levels went down to 3.7 then 3.6 and 3.5. The level did not drop after that.

All afternoon I had visitors. Christopher was there with Lily. Lily was eleven months old. She was walking holding on to everything, including walls. However, she wouldn't let go and walk on her own. She was very entertaining for she wore shoes that squeaked. She looked like a little windup doll. Lois Jane, Kenny, Richard, Jack, Paul, and Carolyn were in the waiting room. They took turns visiting me. Little Lily kept them from becoming too bored.

I was given an EKG; my heart was fine. But not five minutes later, my heart flipped into A-fib. I asked Paul to get the nurse.

The nurse said, "She is not in A-fib."

Paul said, "She is now."

I said, "Come, listen."

"Well," said the nurse, "Sounds like A-fib to me."

I could always tell when my heart was out. This had been happening for over five months, several times a day and getting worse.

Five p.m. Dr. Olson came in to talk. Paul, Christopher, Kenny and Lois Jane, who was holding Lily were in the room. He said right up front, "I have never done an ablation with blood as thin as 3.5." The highest number he had worked on was 3.1. "If we do this today the chances of bleeding out are much higher. You have a choice – You go home – which means you will have to wait three months before I can do it. I know you are getting worse so that's not a very good option. You can always have another doctor do it, maybe in the next three or four weeks, or I will stay tonight and do it. You have to make the decision."

I looked at Paul and then at Christopher. "What should I do?"

I asked the doctor, "What is the worst thing that you can see happening with my case today?"

"Bleeding," He answered.

"Will it kill me?"

"No, we can stop the bleeding . . . and it will take a little longer for you to recover."

Now What?

Christopher said, "Every time I talk to you on the phone I can tell you are getting worse, Mom. There are always risks to every surgery, but you have the best doctor in Indy, which makes a big difference."

Paul said, "I hate to take you back home."

"Then let's do it." When you like your doctor, it makes it easier to go ahead and make that decision. Since January of this year, I have seen six heart specialists. Everyone had his or her own specialties, but Dr. Olson was my favorite. He even bought my book. His wife sent a card telling me she enjoyed reading it. I didn't want another doctor to do my procedure. I wanted Dr. Olson. What he did next sealed the deal.

"Let's all have a prayer now," he said. He held Paul's hand, then Christopher's. Kenny and Lois Jane were in on it as well. Kenny led the prayer, for Paul was far too emotional. Paul stayed strong for me and I know that was very hard for him to do. Then Christopher hugged me and Paul kissed me goodbye.

I was on my way.

The nurses pushed me on my gurney through empty hallways and abandoned nurse stations. I asked, "Where is everyone?"

"Gone home," they answered.

Dr. Olson was doing a special operation for me. In others words, he was working late. We stopped outside the operating room. I walked in. Something about keeping the room sterile. I looked around; it really didn't look like an operating room. It was more like a very clean storage room. Chairs were lined up on the right side of the room. Several computers lined the walls. There was a step for me to use to get up on the operating table. The table had a light disposable air mattress filled with hot air. It felt warm, for the room was ice cold.

There were three people, one male, and two females preparing for whatever was going to take place next. They did not have masks, gloves, or white gowns. The process of stuffing me into the table began. Egg carton foam was used to fill up any extra space. Hundreds of wires, different colors, and different numbers were laid on top of me. The brown number six was missing. Found it. I was laying on it.

My arms were placed to my sides. Egg carton foam was used to fill up any extra space, for they did not want me to move.

"Are you comfortable?" I was asked. "You are going to be here for a long time."

They shackled my wrist and my feet. I asked, "Do you have a key for those?" They thought that was funny. I was looking closely around me, for I thought I might put this in my book. I told them the only reason I was here was to do research for my book. They gave me ideas like

"Torture chamber" or maybe "The return of Mrs. Frankenstein."

The anesthesiologist guy put a crown on my head. It was metal and it felt like a scratcher that one uses to clean dishes. Then I was hooked up to the computer.

. . . Six hours later, I remember thinking someone was throwing me around and it hurt. "Why do you have to be so rough?" I thought.

"Oh, no!" I thought. "I am in Gettysburg and they don't know I am alive. They are throwing me away. No, they are rushing me down a hallway. I am on a gurney. I was now in a huge concrete room." It sure looked like the hospital parking garage to me. However, I couldn't see well at all. There was this light bulb above me.

I could see Dr. Olson. I heard Paul's voice. Paul put his hand through the side of the gurney. He was turned towards me and I grabbed his hand. If I was going to be in Gettysburg, he was coming to.

I remember saying, "Is it over? Is it over?"

"Yes, Catherine, it is over," answered Paul.

"Do I have my legs? Do I have my legs?"

"Why, yes, dear, you have your legs."

The doctor tried to talk to Paul. He had a hard time turning around because I wouldn't let go of his hand. I held tighter, until my mind told me I was not in Gettysburg. "It is just a dream," I told myself and I went back to sleep.

Now, why did I think I was in Gettysburg? The night before, I watched the History Channel and the special on Gettysburg. My advice to anyone who is to have surgery the next day is to be careful what you put into your brain because it may come back to haunt you.

I was now in recovery and it was 9:30 at night. Paul was by my side. All my visitors waited with Paul all day. It had been a long day, for they stayed virtually for 12 hours. Christopher took Lily to our home, for I was to be released two hours after the procedure. At least that is what we thought.

My blood count was still way too thin. I was not allowed to move. The four catheters used to fix my heart were still in place. They were afraid to remove them because they thought I would bleed out. They kept me in recovery. Because of this, Paul could not stay with me for the night. They took him upstairs to a waiting room.

I tried to sleep, but the nurse came in every hour to take a blood test. In addition, the automatic blood pressure machine went off every 30 minutes. Six hours later, I told the nurse I could not keep still any longer. My back was in spasms and my legs started to jump.

They smiled and said, "We have been waiting for you to ask for something for a long time." They were amazed I waited six hours. I was given morphine every two hours.

Now What?

They allowed Paul back at six a.m. He didn't get any sleep either. My blood was still too thin. After twenty-two hours, they had to give me something to get my blood level up so they could take the catheters out. All that time I could not move.

I could not talk above a whisper, and my throat felt like they left a pair of scissors in there. A camera, tubes and a balloon, that kept saliva from going to my lungs, were all put down my throat. One or more of these things seemed to have nicked the inside of my throat. A bruise started to form on the outside.

My poor husband Paul. The recovery room, which we were still in, had no place but a small chair for Paul to sit. He finally laid his head down on the bed. He never left my side.

Dr. Olson was in and out all day. He was impressed that nine people stayed 12 hours in the waiting room to be with Paul. Dr. Olson watched over me all day.

Finally, they let me sit up. I felt like I had turned to stone. It turns out I gained several pounds overnight. They were pumping the fluids into me all day. The nurse wanted to hold my arm to get me walking. I said, No, thank you, I need Paul's arm." She could take the other one. Paul's arm was already worn in. People didn't realize that I had to use Paul's elbow for six months. I was always so dizzy. The nurse was surprised how well I did.

Paul ordered food. I tried a mouthful of mashed potatoes. But there was no place for it to go down. I managed to eat a Popsicle.

Finally, we were on our way home. I slept most of the hour and a half to get there. Christopher was carrying Lily from the mailbox when we came into the driveway. Very slowly, Paul helped me upstairs to my bed. I stayed upstairs for four days.

I had a lunch date with Lily in my office and she made visits to my room. Paul, Christopher, and Lily took good care of me.

Turns out, I had a terrible bruise on my throat. My whole face was swollen. My head hurt, my ears hurt, and Richard said I looked like I had a goatee.

However, one thing I was so grateful for was that my heart was fixed. No more banging, no more pain.

Many, many friends prayed and cried out to God in my bhalf. God heard and God healed. That was five weeks ago and I feel well. It seems like I have found myself.

*****

Paul and I have just bought a new Ford Escape. We call it the car/truck. Then we bought a popup camper. We are going camping.

God is not done with me yet. Paul will retire in a year or so, and then we plan to start two businesses. He has earned a degree in computer repair and will set up a small business. And with Paul's help, we will begin a publishing company called "Watt Light Publishing Company." I have many books inside my heart and head, just waiting to be put on paper or on Kindle. We want to help other writers to publish their written work. These are two doors that God is opening, and we pray for the faith to pass through.

Thank you for reading my book. If you have any questions or comments, you can contact me at my email address: cawilcoxson@theladycatherinecompany.com or my website: www.theladycatherinecompany.com.

Now What?

Dear God,

I pray for faith. . .

Actually, I pray for more faith. There are days my faith is weak. Help me to be strong. For I know You are always by my side.

Let me not be afraid to go through the doors You open for me.

May this book touch the hearts of those who read it. May it direct them to You, God.

I love You, God.

In Jesus name, I pray.

Catherine

**Orchard Hills Church of Christ Building
Covington, Indiana**

Now What?

The LORD bless you, and keep you; The LORD make His face shine on you, And be gracious to you; The LORD lift up His countenance on you, And give you peace.' [51]

Epilogue: Six Years Later

It is hard to believe how much time has passed since I finished *Open Doors and Open Windows: A Journey with God* six years ago. Lots of things have happened to Paul and me. At the conclusion of the book, I had just experienced a two-catheter ablation for A-fib, a condition I had been plagued with for many years. Finally, something had to be done since my heart was out of rhythm for many hours a day. The procedure to remedy my problem was grueling, but it fixed my heart.

    In the fall of 2011, we purchased our 2009 Ford Escape, which we called a car/truck and then a popup camper, which we planned to take with us on our trip to Nova Scotia in the summer of 2012. Retirement was just one year away, and Paul and I were planning to set up two smaller businesses as subsidiaries of the larger company called The Lady Catherine Company. The first business, Watt Light Publishing Company, would publish my books as well as others' books. The second business, P-LCC Computer Services, would be used by Paul to do computer repair. Paul took a computer course, which gave him credentials needed to do computer repair.

In November of 2011, I had eyelid surgery on both of my eyes. That was another traumatic experience. My eye was completely sewed together, which freaked Paul and me out. Surgery was done on one eye, and then two weeks later, it was done on my other eye. Although the surgery was difficult to go through, I could see well, when it was finished.

Back in 2010, Paul and I went to DeQuincy, Louisiana on vacation to visit Michael and Jennifer's family. While we were in DeQuincy, we purchased a house in anticipation of living there after our retirement in 2012. We had the house painted inside and then rented it out for two years. This arrangement would help pay the upkeep on the house until we were ready to move in. We were enjoying living in Covington, Indiana, and working with the Orchard Hills Church. God blessed with five good years of ministry in Covington. We made many friends there with whom we remain in contact to this day. Paul informed the elders of the Orchard Hills Church a year in advance that we would plan to retire the end of May 2012. Before the date of our actual retirement, Paul and I took most of our household belongings to DeQuincy and stored them in our two buildings on the property where our house was. At the time, we still had a tenant living in our house, but we would not move in until the fall of 2012. Finally, our last day at Orchard Hills came. Paul preached his farewell sermon titled "Farewell to

Epilogue: Six Years Later

Orchard Hills." It was a bittersweet time for Paul and me since we had fallen in love with the members of the congregation. They gave us a send off, which reminded us of going on a honeymoon after a wedding. We got into our car/truck, pulling our popup camper and headed toward Nova Scotia for our three-month book tour to sell my first book entitled *The Adventures of Captain Heman Kenney and Lady Catherine - 1838 - 1917*. More details of our book tour can be found in my latest book, *Don't Forget Maude: The Tale of Two Sisters*.

    After our three-month tour to Nova Scotia, we made our way to our adopted home in DeQuincy, Louisiana. Paul developed a hernia, which caused him a lot of trouble. Consequently, I had to do a lot of the hard work of putting the popup camper up and down each time we stopped at a campground. We were happy to get to DeQuincy. It was like coming home because we had worked here before for seven years. There was no water or electricity hooked up in the house. However, the temperatures were cool enough to open the windows. Paul and I slept on our bed. We weren't going to spend another night in that popup camper. We'd already spent 80 + nights in that camper. We sold it not long after.

    Paul had his hernia taken care of. After his recovery, we began working on our house. We moved walls, enlarging the dining room and kitchen. The whole family and friends worked on this. It is an ongoing project.

    Since our return to DeQuincy, Paul and I have experienced some sad times. My mother, Doris, passed away in 2013. We made a trip back to Nova Scotia for her funeral. Our son Christopher came from Cincinnati, Ohio to attend his grandmother's funeral as well. Needless to say, it was a sad time, but we rejoice that her suffering ended, and she went to be with the Lord. Not long after that, Paul's brother Robert passed away in Decatur, Alabama. Again, we traveled to attend a funeral for a loved one. Robert was a Christian too, so we're confident he is in the arms of His Lord as well.

Paul was able to set up his computer business, which he continues to this day. He keeps an advertisement in the local newspaper offering his services as a computer technician. As for me, I continued to write my next book, *Don't Forget Maude: The Tale of Two Sisters*. We have worshiped with the DeQuincy Church of Christ, where Paul was asked to serve as one of the elders. To serve as an elder was a goal Paul had for a long time. In addition to Paul's duties as an elder, Paul and I have taught Bible classes and served in other areas where we have been needed. A couple times a month Paul preaches for a small congregation called Lone Pine 30 miles from DeQuincy.

Paul and I had hoped to spend our retirement years in a quiet and unassuming manner, serving the Lord in the DeQuincy area and enjoying our children and grandchildren, but that was not to be. The day after Christmas, three years ago this December, the awful phone call came. Our only son, Christopher, the son of our love, had been arrested for a terrible mistake that will haunt him the rest of his life. His court-appointed lawyer tried repeatedly to get the charges reduced, but the prosecutor wouldn't have it. It ended in Christopher making a plea-bargain, resulting in a prison sentence of 18 years.

Epilogue: Six Years Later

Needless to say, we were crushed beyond measure, and our hearts were broken. Since that time, Paul and I have cried an ocean of tears. We begged and pleaded with God over and over to intervene in the situation, but He seemed to have other plans.

Perhaps you remember the account of King David in the Old Testament, who committed adultery with Bathsheba, had her husband Uriah murdered, tried to cover it up, then repented of his sin, was forgiven by God but had to live with the consequences. In a similar manner, Christopher repented of his sin and has been forgiven, but he has to live with the consequences. Since Christopher's incarceration, he is making a life for himself in prison. He is proclaiming the gospel of Jesus, participating in and conducting Bible classes, and living his Christian life in the prison. Christopher is known as the "prayer man." The other inmates know Christopher is a genuine Christian, and they are attracted to him. As a result, Paul and I have become involved with some of the inmates whose lives have been touched by Christopher. Because of that, we have visited with some of those inmates during our visits to see Christopher. Likewise, some of the ladies of the DeQuincy church are involved in sending cards, letters, and other things to some of those inmates. I guess you could say God has taken a bad, and terrible thing and turned it into an effort to advance His cause and kingdom, even within that prison where Christopher is. Our hearts have healed partially, but our lives and the lives of Christopher's family will never again be the same.

During our visits to visit Christopher, Paul and I have been blessed to visit with our little grandchildren, Lily and

Henry and their mother. But they have since moved to another state, so our chances to visit them now will be harder. We do get to visit them via Skype occasionally.

Two years ago in June 2015, Paul had the privilege of making a two-week mission trip to Ghana, West Africa with a mission team. It was very eye-opening for Paul, and very eventful because nearly 100 individuals professed faith in Jesus and were immersed into Jesus for the forgiveness of their sins. Those people touched Paul's life, and theirs were touched by his. Even now Paul remains in contact with some of the Christians there through Facebook.

After the awful tragedy with Christopher, Paul and I had hoped we would be spared further heartache for a while, but not so. The day after New Year's Day this year, 2017, I woke up with my breast swollen three times its size. I knew I had a problem, but was unsure of its extent. The next day we went to Urgent Care to get me checked out. Tests revealed I had cancer. Further tests showed I have fourth-stage breast cancer. That means the cancer has metastasized, spread to other places in my body, including my lymph nodes, right lung, and tenth vertebrae in my back. Doctors say the cancer can be treated, but there is no cure. So now I'm involved in chemotherapy to try to kill cancer cells and put me into remission. Chemo and its side effects are hard to endure, but with the Lord's help, we will continue on. Many people all over Canada, the United States, in the prison where Christopher is, and indeed other parts of the world are praying for me and Paul. Paul and I have been

Epilogue: Six Years Later

touched by the outpouring of love and support, prayers, cards, phone calls, and well-wishes from so many people.

What the future holds for me on this earth, I don't know. Sometimes it is hard to make it through the day. But Paul and I are using this time to read and study God's Word and other Christian literature, pray, sing to the Lord, and do whatever we can within the confines of my illness. As long as the Lord allows me to live, I will serve Him alongside my husband Paul until He calls me to glory. In the meantime, we will spend time with Michael, Jennifer, our three grandsons, and our church family in the DeQuincy church. Whenever I am able, we will visit Christopher and some of the inmates in prison.

Open Doors and Open Windows: Journey with God

House In DeQuincy

Epilogue: Six Years Later

**Paul and Catherine
42 Wedding Anniversary**

Endnotes

[1] Matthew 11:28-30.

[2] Matthew 7:7

[3] 2 Peter 1:5-9

[4] Romans 5:1-5

[5] Isaiah 59:2

[6] James 1:14-15

[7] Malachi 2:16,

[8] Romans 8:28.

[9] John 3:16

[10] 1 Corinthians 13:1-13

[11] 3 John 3

[12] Job 2:13

[13] Written by Text: Charlotte Elliott, 1789-1871; Music: William B. Bradbury, 1816-1868. In the public domain.

[14] 2 Corinthians 3:5

[15] Romans 5:8

[16] Romans 3: 23

[17] 1 Timothy 3:11

[18] 1 Timothy 3:11

[19] Matthew 19:13-14

[20] STAY IN YOUR OWN BACK YARD (aka Mama's Little Alabama Coon)(Lyn Udall / Karl Kennett) - 1899

[21] Acts 17:24-28

[22] 1 Peter 1:5-7

[23] Phillipians 4:11 (NASB).

[24] Psalm 46:10.

[25] Matthew 25 14:30.

[26] Acts 11:14.

[27] Acts 18:8.

[28] 1 Corinthians 16:15.

[29] Acts 22:16

[30] 1 Peter 3:21.

[31] The proceeding came from John 4.

[32] John 11.

[33] Taken from the Gospel of Mark.

[34] John 11.

[35] A compilation taken from Gospel accounts.

[36] Revelation 1:18.

[37] 1 John 5:13-16.

---

[38] 1 Corinthians 15:54-57.

[39] Colloquialisms for Canadian $1.00 and $2.00 coins.

[40] Boats used by Cajun people.

[41] Matthew 15:1-3

[42] Mark 7:6-9

[43] 2 Thessalonians 2:15

[44] 2 Thessalonians 2:5

[45] A compilation from the Gospel accounts in the New Testament.

[46] John 3:1-2

[47] John 3:1-21.

[48] Daniel 5:1-30.

[49] Hebrews 13:5-6.

[50] Ephesians 3:4-6.

[51] Num 6:24-26 (NASB)

www.ingramcontent.com/pod-product-compliance
Lightning Source LLC
Chambersburg PA
CBHW071152300426
44113CB00009B/1177